CliffsNotes™

White's
The Once and Future King

By Daniel Moran

IN THIS BOOK

- Learn about the Life and Background of the Author
- Preview an Introduction to the Novel
- Explore themes, character development, and recurring images in the Critical Commentaries
- Examine in-depth Character Analyses
- Acquire an understanding of the novel with a Critical Essay
- Reinforce what you learn with CliffsNotes Review
- Find additional information to further your study in CliffsNotes Resource Center and online at www.cliffsnotes.com

IDG Books Worldwide,
An International Data Group Company
Foster City, CA • Chicago, IL • Indianapolis, IN • New York, NY

About the Author

Daniel Moran is an award-winning high-school teacher who has been teaching *The Once and Future King* for years.

Publisher's Acknowledgments

Editorial

Project Editor: Tere Drenth

Acquisitions Editor: Gregory W. Tubach

Glossary Editors: The editors and staff of Webster's New World Dictionaries

Editorial Administrator: Michelle Hacker

Production

Indexer: York Production Services, Inc.

Proofreader: York Production Services, Inc.

IDG Books Indianapolis Production Department

CliffsNotes White's *The Once and Future King*

Published by

IDG Books Worldwide, Inc.

An International Data Group Company

919 E. Hillsdale Blvd.

Suite 400

Foster City, CA 94404

www.idgbooks.com (IDG Books Worldwide Web site)

www.cliffsnotes.com (CliffsNotes Web site)

ISBN: 0-7645-8550-9

Printed in the United States of America

10 9 8 7 6 5 4 3 2 1

1O/TR/QV/QQ/IN

Distributed in the United States by IDG Books Worldwide, Inc.

Library of Congress Cataloging-in-Publication Data

Moran, Daniel.

CliffsNotes, White's The Once and Future King / by Daniel Moran.

p. cm.

Includes bibliographical references and index.

ISBN 0-7645-8550-9 (alk. paper)

1. White, T.H. (Terence Hanbury), 1906-1964. Once and Future King--Examinations--Study guides. 2. Arthurian romances--Adaptations--Examinations--Study guides. I. Title: Once and Future King.

PR6045.H2. O536 2000

823'.912--dc21   00–035027

                                                                CIP

Distributed by CDG Books Canada Inc. for Canada; by Transworld Publishers Limited in the United Kingdom; by IDG Norge Books for Norway; by IDG Sweden Books for Sweden; by IDG Books Australia Publishing Corporation Pty. Ltd. for Australia and New Zealand; by TransQuest Publishers Pte Ltd. for Singapore, Malaysia, Thailand, Indonesia, and Hong Kong; by Gotop Information Inc. for Taiwan; by ICG Muse, Inc. for Japan; by Intersoft for South Africa; by Eyrolles for France; by International Thomson Publishing for Germany, Austria and Switzerland; by Distribuidora Cuspide for Argentina; by LR International for Brazil; by Galileo Libros for Chile; by Ediciones ZETA S.C.R. Ltda. for Peru; by WS Computer Publishing Corporation, Inc., for the Philippines; by Contemporanea de Ediciones for Venezuela; by Express Computer Distributors for the Caribbean and West Indies; by Micronesia Media Distributor, Inc. for Micronesia; by Chips Computadoras S.A. de C.V. for Mexico; by Editorial Norma de Panama S.A. for Panama; by American Bookshops for Finland.

For general information on IDG Books Worldwide's books in the U.S., please call our Consumer Customer Service department at **800-762-2974.** For reseller information, including discounts and premium sales, please call our Reseller Customer Service department at **800-434-3422.**

For information on where to purchase IDG Books Worldwide's books outside the U.S., please contact our International Sales department at **317-596-5530** or fax **317-572-4002.**

For consumer information on foreign language translations, please contact our Customer Service department at **800-434-3422,** fax 317-572-4002, or e-mail rights@idgbooks.com.

For information on licensing foreign or domestic rights, please phone **650-653-7098.**

For sales inquiries and special prices for bulk quantities, please contact our Order Services department at **800-434-3422** or write to the address above.

For information on using IDG Books Worldwide's books in the classroom or for ordering examination copies, please contact our Educational Sales department at **800-434-2086** or fax **317-572-4005.**

For press review copies, author interviews, or other publicity information, please contact our Public Relations department at **650-653-7000** or fax **650-653-7500.**

For authorization to photocopy items for corporate, personal, or educational use, please contact Copyright Clearance Center, 222 Rosewood Drive, Danvers, MA 01923, or fax **978-750-4470.**

Table of Contents

How to Use This Book

CliffsNotes *The Once and Future King* supplements the original work, giving you background information about the author, an introduction to the novel, a graphical character map, critical commentaries, expanded glossaries, and a comprehensive index. CliffsNotes Review tests your comprehension of the original text and reinforces learning with questions and answers, practice projects, and more. For further information on T.H. White and *The Once and Future King*, check out the CliffsNotes Resource Center.

CliffsNotes provides the following icons to highlight essential elements of particular interest:

Reveals the underlying themes in the work.

Helps you to more easily relate to or discover the depth of a character.

Uncovers elements such as setting, atmosphere, mystery, passion, violence, irony, symbolism, tragedy, foreshadowing, and satire.

Enables you to appreciate the nuances of words and phrases.

Don't Miss Our Web Site

Discover classic literature as well as modern-day treasures by visiting the CliffsNotes Web site at www.cliffsnotes.com. You can obtain a quick download of a CliffsNotes title, purchase a title in print form, browse our catalog, or view online samples.

You'll also find interactive tools that are fun and informative, links to interesting Web sites, tips, articles, and additional resources to help you, not only for literature, but for test prep, finance, careers, computers, and Internet, too. See you at www.cliffsnotes.com!

LIFE AND BACKGROUND OF THE AUTHOR

Personal Background

An Unhappy Childhood

Terrence Hanbury (T.H.) White was born in Bombay, India, on May 29, 1906. The only child of Garrick White, a district superintendent of police, and Constance Aston White, the daughter of an Indian judge, he was born eighteen months into what he would later describe as his parents' doomed marriage. White's father's career kept him on the move; his often-neglected son became ill at the age of eleven and was ordered, by a doctor, to be removed to England. After a year, Garrick returned to India; eighteen months later, Constance followed him.

White stayed with his grandparents and was enrolled in Cheltenham College, a traditional school that dated to the Victorian era. White found the school more like a prison than a haven from his awful home life. According to White's diary, the housemaster was a "sadistic middle-aged bachelor with a gloomy suffused [blushing] face," while the prefects (senior pupils who helped discipline the younger boys) were "lithe and brighter copies" of the housemaster who used "to beat us after evening prayers."

As the reader of *The Sword in the Stone* (the first volume of *The Once and Future King*) may infer, White realized that education cannot happen if it is only associated with physical punishment—something to which Merlyn, in the novel, never resorts.

Cambridge and Italy

The one bright spot of White's time at Cheltenham was his meeting of a master named C. F. Scott, who praised White's talent and encouraged him to be a writer. Because of this, White often attested that he would "be grateful to him till I die." In 1923, White's parents obtained a divorce; the following year, White left Cheltenham and spent a year doing private tutoring in order to afford the tuition at Cambridge, where he enrolled in 1925.

White found Cambridge much more to his liking. It was there that he met the man whom he would call "the great literary influence in my life," L. J. Potts, one of his tutors who, ironically, White initially "disliked to the point of rage for about a year." White faced another hardship, however, when he contracted tuberculosis in 1927 and spent four months in a sanitarium. Potts raised enough money to send White to Italy to recuperate; it was there that White composed his first novel (although it was not his first published work), *They Wintered Abroad*. In 1929, White moved back to England, where his first book, *Loved Helen and Other Poems*, was published. The volume was favorably received, although he made no great impressions as a young Eliot or Auden. He graduated from Cambridge (with distinction) that same year, and for the next six years (1930–1936) he taught at different academies and published seven books, among them a murder-mystery (*Dead Mr. Nixon*), an experimental historical novel (*Farewell Victoria*), and a philosophical yet slapstick comedy (*Earth Stopped*). In 1936, White compiled and edited *England Have My Bones*, a memoir taken directly from White's own daybooks in which he recounts his life between March 3, 1934 and the same day a year later. The book, a collection of anecdotes and scenes about White's hunting, fishing, and piloting experiences (mixed with some philosophical speculation), was a bestseller and allowed White to resign from teaching in order to devote himself full-time to writing.

White, Malory, and *Le Morte D'Arthur*

While living in a gamekeeper's cottage near Stowe School, where he served as head of the English department until his resignation in 1936, White reread Sir Thomas Malory's *Le Morte D'Arthur*, the fifteenth-century chronicle of King Arthur, his Round Table, and the quest for the Holy Grail. Reading Malory purely for pleasure (rather than for an assignment) made White look at the Arthurian myth in a new light; he found the story exciting and relevant to modern life. White was unable to shake off its allure; in a letter dated January 14, 1938, he wrote to Potts, his tutor: "I was thrilled and astonished to find (a) that the thing was a perfect tragedy, with a beginning, a middle and an end implicit in the beginning, and (b) that the characters were real people with recognizable reactions which could be forecast . . . It is more or less a kind of wish-fulfillment of the kind of things I should have liked to have happened to me when I was a boy."

Later that year, White published his "wish-fulfillment" as *The Sword in the Stone*. It was selected as a main selection of the Book of the Month Club and received glowing reviews. Writing in *The New Statesman*, David Garnett called it "the most delightful book for old and young";

Vida D. Scudder, writing in *The Atlantic Monthly*, remarked, "If you are a boy, you can find here the best battles and enchantments going. If you are a serious-minded adult, you will savor the suggestions of an advanced educational theory."

The Once and Future King

Motivated by *The Sword in the Stone*'s success, White moved to Ireland in 1939 and immediately began work on a sequel, *The Witch in the Wood* (later titled *The Queen of Air and Darkness*). Like its predecessor, *The Witch in the Wood* was favorably reviewed, although some critics found the story of Arthur battling rebellious Gaels less effective and more tedious than *The Sword in the Stone*. Writing in *The New Yorker*, for example, Clifton Faidman argued that "the novelty of [White's] special brand of humor, that of anachronism [is] pretty well exhausted by the first book." Still, White continued his romance with the Arthurian myth and, in 1940, released *The Ill-Made Knight*, his study of Lancelot and Guenever's adultery. Beatrice Sherman, writing in *The New York Times*, called this installment "a more thoughtful, adult and subdued piece of writing" than its two predecessors.

It was not, however, until 1958 that *The Sword in the Stone, The Queen of Air and Darkness,* and *The Ill-Made Knight* appeared together in *The Once and Future King*, along with a concluding volume, *The Candle in the Wind*. After *The Once and Future King* was finally released, readers on both sides of the Atlantic praised White's grandiose and accessible retelling of Malory's story. *The Once and Future King* proved so successful that the rights to it were bought by Alan Jay Lerner and Frederick Lowe—the Broadway musical team responsible for *Brigadoon* and *My Fair Lady*—who turned White's novels into the 1960 musical spectacular, *Camelot*. Although White had nothing to do with the production, he approved of and enjoyed it. (The play was made into a film in 1967.) In 1963, Disney released an animated version of *The Sword in the Stone*.

The Book of Merlyn, which White had intended as the fifth installment of his series, was not published until 1977. According to John Mullin, who reviewed the novel for the journal *America*, World War II was responsible for the delay in the book's release: White's pacifism (as well as the paper shortage) ruined its marketability. Mullin notes in his review that this fifth volume of the story differs from the first four in its "*saeve indignatio*, a fury at the persistently cruel and pompous human race, which White expresses through argument and satire rather than romance." *The Book of Merlyn* is an interesting curiosity that reveals White's anger at what he saw as the violent and heartless world that surrounded him.

Last Years

After moving to Italy in 1962, White wrote at a less frenetic pace than he had during the war years. He began an American lecture tour, however, in which he delivered a very Merlyn-like talk on "The Pleasures of Learning" and another on Hadrian, the Roman Emperor who constructed a famous wall of defense in England. White died of heart failure on a Mediterranean cruise on January 17, 1964; he was buried in Athens near Hadrian's Arch. 1965 saw the publication of *America at Last: The American Journal of White*, which recounted his American lecture tour.

INTRODUCTION TO THE NOVEL

Introduction

In his *Reflections on the Revolution in France* (1790), Edmund Burke, the Irish philosopher and statesman, describes his disappointment in how the French thought of Marie Antoinette, their Queen: "I thought ten thousand swords must have leaped from their scabbards to avenge even a look that threatened her with insult. But the age of chivalry is gone. That of sophisters, economists and calculators has succeeded; and the glory of Europe is gone forever."

Like many of his contemporaries, Burke had read Malory's *Le Morte D'Arthur*, a collection of tales and exploits of England's greatest and most world-renown figure: King Arthur. Burke assumes that his reader will immediately understand what he means by "chivalry": defending the honor of a royal woman by means of physical force. This idea of stouthearted men defending helpless ladies—along with the ideals of the Round Table and the Quest for the Holy Grail—may be somewhat clichéd in the twenty-first century, rooted in an imaginary past. Yet these ideas are still very much a part of our experience and culture, and an examination of the Arthurian myth can help clarify the historical and literary sources of such thinking.

Was There a Real King Arthur?

While some modern Americans may think of Great Britain as the cradle of refined, European civilization, medieval Britain was a violent and war-torn place marked by endless invasions, broken alliances, and defeated hopes. Although the Romans intended to stabilize the borders of Briton (and subdue its population of Celts), by 407, the Empire had completely withdrawn all of its forces in order to defend its own interests in Italy. This left Britain a self-governed, yet chaotic, island, and without the Roman legions to defend them, the Britons found themselves under constant attack from different bands of pagan invaders. Picts attacked from the north (present-day Scotland) and Scotts attacked from the west (present-day Northern Ireland). 446 marked the Anglo-Saxon invasion, when hordes of Germanic warriors swept into the island. According to David Day, author of *The Search for King Arthur*, "If ever a people needed a champion, it was the Britons of the late fifth century." The Britons needed a leader who could unite their forces against the constant threats of invasion.

Such a leader was found in a Romanized Briton named Artorius—
"Arthur" in its British form—who led the Britons to victory against the
Saxon, Pict, Scot, and Irish hordes. Also known as the Dux Bellorum
or "Duke of Battles," Artoris made such an impression on the Britons—
and on their enemies—that he became a symbol of strength, defiance,
and bravery. Over time, Artoris the Dux Bellorum, was transformed
into the legendary King Arthur found in poetry, prose, theater, and film.
Although he did not pull a sword from a stone or create a real Round
Table, Artoris, through his military prowess, created something much
more lasting: a legendary figure that has come to embody all of England's virtues, much in the same way that Superman has done for the
United States.

Arthur in Literature

Although the legends of King Arthur had existed for hundreds of
years in ballads and popular folk songs, it was not until 1135 that the
first extensive biography of Arthur was written. This first recounting of
Arthur's life appears in *The History of the Kings of Britain*, a pseudo-his-
torical work written by a Norman cleric known as Geoffrey of Mon-
mouth (about 1100–1154). Geoffrey's version of the myth lays the
groundwork for future versions: He mentions Arthur's father, Uther
Pendragon, his marriage to Guenever (who, in *The History of the Kings
of Britain*, is the daughter of a Roman nobleman), and the king's
betrayal by Mordred. However, Geoffrey also adds that Arthur seized
Paris and almost conquered all of Rome, were it not for the fact that
the treachery of Mordred called him back to Britain to fight against the
usurper. As Shakespeare did with some of his history plays, Geoffrey
reconstrued "history" into a story with a clear political agenda: in this
case, to use the life of Arthur as a way to justify the idea that the Norman French were destined to become a force as great as the Roman
Empire.

The most famous account of Arthur's life, however, is one written
by Sir Thomas Malory (about 1410–1471). A criminal who often found
himself in jail, Malory was nonetheless gifted with a fantastic imagination that allowed him to compile different versions of the Arthurian
myth and shape them into a sometimes uneven but overall coherent
whole. His *Le Morte D'Arthur* ("The Death of Arthur") was written—
in prison—between March of 1469 and March of 1470. Using the Vul-
gate Cycle, a thirteenth century compilation of Old French tales of

Lancelot, the Quest for the Grail, and the death of Arthur, Malory fashioned a book so popular that it was one of the first books printed in England. The printer, William Caxton (about 1422–1491) is now believed to have freely edited Malory's book in order to make his separate tales fit into more of a whole. (The book's only surviving manuscript was found in 1934 and was not written in Malory's hand.) Caxton's introduction to *Le Morte D'Arthur* reveals his moral (as opposed to financial) intentions in publishing the book: "I . . . present this book following; which I have emprised to imprint; and treateth of the noble acts, feats of arms of chivalry, prowess, hardiness, humanity, love, courtesy and very gentleness, with many wonderful histories and adventures."

Le Morte D'Arthur is at once a tumultuous adventure story and a guide to chivalric ideals. Its characters constantly attempt to live by the codes of chivalry—a system of beliefs that holds that the strong must defend the weak; a knight must struggle to maintain his purity; and that the individual must subsume his own desires and even his identity—under the wings of a greater good. Malory's book begins with the betrayal of Cornwall by Uther Pendragon, Arthur's father, and ends with the death of Arthur at the hands of Mordred, Arthur's ill-conceived son. In its pages can be found the now-famous stories of Arthur pulling the sword from the stone, the Quest for the Holy Grail, and the adultery of Lancelot and Guenever. All of these tales serve as moral instruction as well as inspiring reading. Like many other epics, *Le Morte D'Arthur* features a central figure who desperately tries to maintain his ideals despite the constant threats to undo them. Also like many mythical figures, he falls because of his own actions (conceiving Mordred with his half-sister, Morgan Le Fay) and is destroyed because of an event that occurred far in his past.

Since Malory's time, many other writers have shown an interest in the Arthurian myth. The Puritan poet John Milton considered the Arthurian myth as the basis for an epic poem, but eventually decided to use Adam and Eve (the result was *Paradise Lost*). The Victorian poet Alfred, Lord Tennyson reworked many of the legends into his *Idylls of the King*; Mark Twain saw the legends as a means by which he could satirize his contemporaries and composed *A Connecticut Yankee in King Arthur's Court*. The twenty-first century is showing a great resurgence of Arthurian literature and scholarship: Novelists still draw on the Arthurian legends for inspiration, and universities widely offer courses in Arthurian literature. Although King Arthur is forever associated with

England, the values he struggles to preserve and the conflicts he faces are universal, making him a figure with worldwide appeal.

A Brief Synopsis of *The Sword in the Stone*

The first volume of *The Once and Future King, The Sword in the Stone*, begins as the Wart, an innocent and wholesome boy living in twelfth-century England, is informed by his adoptive father, Sir Ector, that he must begin his education. While wandering in the Forest Sauvage after a night of adventure with King Pellinore (who hunts for the Questing Beast), the Wart chances upon the cottage of Merlyn, an old magician who "lives backward" through time and thus possesses the ability to know the future. Merlyn informs the Wart that he will become his tutor and accompanies him back to Sir Ector's Castle of the Forest Sauvage. After reviewing the wizard's references, Sir Ector hires the old magician. Kay, the Wart's older brother, becomes jealous over the Wart's fortune, as he does throughout the novel.

Merlyn's lessons consist of transforming the Wart into different kinds of animals. The boy's first transformation is into a perch, and while swimming in the castle's moat, he meets Mr. P., a ruthless tyrant who talks to him about power. At different points in the novel, the Wart becomes a hawk, an ant, an owl, a wild goose, and a badger: Each animal reveals to the Wart a different way of life, political philosophy, or attitude toward war. Merlyn also has his pupil witness a tilting match (or joust) between King Pellinore and Sir Grummore, where the two men reveal their absurd need to follow the rules of sportsmanlike combat.

Feeling sorry for Kay, the Wart asks Merlyn if he can transform his older brother into an animal as well; the magician explains that he cannot (since that is not what Merlyn was sent for). However, Merlyn does tell the Wart that he and his brother should follow a certain path into the Forest Sauvage, where they will surely find an adventure. The boys do just that and eventually meet Robin Wood, the famous outlaw (often called, in error, "Robin Hood") who explains to the boys that a band of fairies, the Oldest Ones of All led by the witch Morgan Le Fay, have kidnapped his companion, Friar Tuck, and the Dog Boy, one of Sir Ector's servants. The boys agree to help Robin and his men storm the Castle Chariot (a fortress made entirely of food) where the captives are being held. After rescuing the men, Kay kills the *griffin* (a creature with an eagle's head and wings and a lion's body) that guards the castle.

Sir Ector receives a letter from Uther Pendragon, the King of England, informing Sir Ector that the King is sending Sir William Twyti, his royal huntsman, to the Forest Sauvage to kill some wild boars. Sir Ector is expected to receive and care for Twyti and his retinue during his stay. When Twyti arrives, Sir Ector gives a great Christmas feast in which songs are sung and Sir Ector delivers a warm speech. At the boar hunt, the prey is killed but Beaumont, Twyti's favorite hound, is paralyzed from the waist down. While Twyti holds him in his arms, Robin kills the dog to free it from pain. King Pellinore then happens upon the Questing Beast, which has become sick with longing for her once-fanatic hunter, and King Pellinore vows to resume the chase.

Six years pass. Kay prepares for his impending knighthood while the Wart continues his education. (The Wart will become Kay's squire after he is knighted.) King Pellinore informs Sir Ector, Sir Grummore, and Kay that Uther Pendragon has died without an heir, and to remedy this politically chaotic situation, a sword has appeared outside a church in London, running through an anvil and into a stone. The inscription on the sword's pommel reads, "Whoso Pulleth Out This Sword of the Stone and Anvil, is Rightwise King Born of All England." A tournament is announced on New Year's Day to give all able men in England a chance to remove the sword. Kay convinces his father that they should attend, and he agrees. The Wart then enters, upset at Merlyn's announcement that he will no longer be tutoring him. Merlyn does assure the boy, however, that they will meet again.

During the tournament, Kay arrives at the tilting fields and realizes he has forgotten his sword; He orders the Wart to return to their inn and retrieve it. Finding the inn locked and nobody there, the Wart searches for a replacement. He eventually spies the sword in the stone and, and after a short struggle and the guidance of some animal friends, removes it, not realizing the significance of such an action. He returns to the tournament and tells Kay where he found the sword; Kay then lies to Sir Ector and claims that he pulled it from the stone. When they all go back to the stone, however, Kay admits his falsehood and, with his father, falls prostrate before the Wart, hailing him as King. The Wart, confused and embarrassed, bursts into tears.

Eventually, the Wart overcomes his awkwardness with his new title and is given a great party for his coronation. All of the characters offer him gifts. Merlyn reappears and tells the Wart that his real father was Uther Pendragon. He further informs the Wart that, in the future, it will be his "glorious doom" to "take up the burden" of his nobility. After promising to stay with the Wart for a long time, Merlyn addresses him as King Arthur.

List of Characters in *The Sword in the Stone*

The Castle of the Forest Sauvage and Its Environs

The Wart A foundling raised by Sir Ector at the Castle of the Forest Sauvage. Naive and innocent, he undergoes an education at the hands of Merlyn. "The Wart" is a nickname for "Art," and the Wart eventually becomes King Arthur.

Sir Ector The Wart and Kay's father and a kind, good-humored landowner who is Lord of the Castle of the Forest Sauvage.

Kay Sir Ector's eldest (and only natural) son. His stubbornness and craving for honor are revealed in many of his words and actions.

Merlyn A wise and sometimes absent-minded magician who oversees the Wart's education. He lives "backward" in time, moving from the future to the past.

Sir Grummore Grummursum A friend and drinking companion of Sir Ector. He offers King Pellinore a "feather bed" so that he can retire from his hunt for the Questing Beast.

Ralph Passelewe An old man, almost blind and almost deaf, who delights Sir Ector's guests with his racy song at the Christmas feast.

Uther Pendragon The demanding Norman King of all England. At the end of the novel, the Wart learns that Pendragon is his father.

Sir William Twyti Uther Pendragon's royal huntsman, sent to the Castle of the Forest Sauvage to hunt wild boar. He reveals (at one point) his tender side after losing one of his hounds in a hunt.

King Pellinore A wholly comical figure, King Pellinore hunts after the Questing Beast (or "Beast Glatisant") and also participates in an absurd joust with Sir Grummore Grummursum.

Wat An old and crazy man without a nose who lives in the Forest Sauvage. After being pelted with stones by some children, he caught one of the boys (the Dog Boy) and bit off his nose.

The Dog Boy Sir Ector's servant in charge of his kennels and hounds. As a child, he had his nose bitten off by Wat. Later in the novel, he and Wat are reconciled and become friends.

Hob Sir Ector's servant in charge of the mews, where his hawks and falcons are kept.

The Boys' Adventure with Robin Wood

Robin Wood The real name of the legendary Robin Hood, a Saxon thief who defends the poor and who patrols the Forest Sauvage. He is an expert bowman and woodsman.

Maid Marian Robin Wood's wife, who excels in tracking and hunting.

John Naylor A giant of a man (nicknamed "Little John"), John Naylor acts as one of Robin wood's sentries by guarding the giant tree in the Forest Sauvage that Robin uses as a lookout point.

Much A tiny, mute hunchback, who, like John Naylor, serves as one of Robin Wood's sentries.

The Oldest Ones of All The name given to a band of gluttonous fairies who possess the knowledge of the ancient Gaels. Also called the "Old Ones," "Blessed Ones," "Good Folk," and "People of Peace," they, with the help of Morgan Le Fay, kidnap Friar Tuck and the Dog Boy.

Friar Tuck A fried of Robin, taken prisoner by the Oldest Ones of All.

Morgan Le Fay A slug-like witch who, in league with the Oldest Ones of All, kidnaps Friar Tuck and the Dog Boy.

Animals Met by the Wart

Cavall The Wart's favorite hound, cared for by the Dog Boy.

Archimedes Merlyn's owl, who teaches the Wart to fly before sending him off to live with the wild geese.

Mr. P. A tyrannical perch who lords over all the fish in the moat of the Castle of the Forest Sauvage.

Cully A favorite hawk of the Wart and Kay; when the Wart becomes a hawk, he learns that Cully is a colonel among the hawks and has a violent temper.

Balan and Balin Two falcons who befriend the Wart when he becomes a hawk.

Madam A falcon in charge of the mews who interrogates the Wart.

Lyo-lyok A wild goose who teaches the Wart about migration; she is shocked to hear the Wart speak so nonchalantly about war.

The badger The last animal the Wart befriends, the badger is a philosopher who reads the thesis for his doctor's degree to him: It explores why Man has been given, by God, the Order of Dominion over all other animals.

Character Map of *The Sword in the Stone*

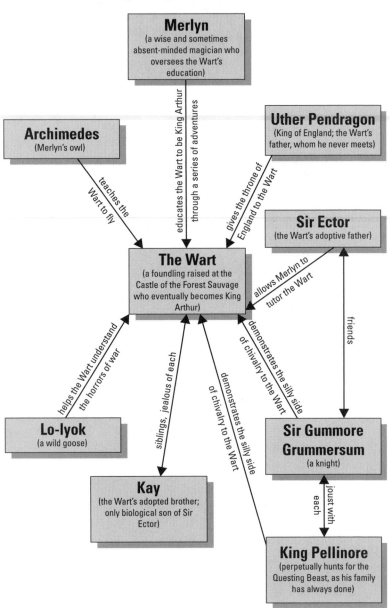

CRITICAL COMMENTARIES

The Sword in the Stone
Chapters 1–5

Summary

The *Sword in the Stone*, the first volume of *The Once and Future King* begins in the Merry England of the Middle Ages, although England is also known throughout the novel as "Gramarye." In Sir Ector's Castle of the Forest Sauvage, Sir Ector and his friend, Sir Grummore, discuss the need for a tutor to "eddicate" Sir Ector's son (Kay) and ward (Art, nicknamed "the Wart"). Sir Ector decides to advertise for a tutor. After their chore of hay-making has been postponed due to rain, the two boys decide to go hawking in the Forest Sauvage, an immense wooded area that surrounds Sir Ector's castle. Cully, a prize hawk, escapes from Kay's grasp and Kay leaves the forest; the Wart stays and considers how to get Cully down from his high perch.

As darkness falls on the Forest Sauvage, the Wart is terrified when an arrow flies at him from an unseen assailant. However, Wart learns that the arrow was not intended for him; instead, it was shot by King Pellinore, who prowls the Forest Sauvage in search of the Beast Glatisant (or "Questing Beast"). Before his clumsy and comical departure, King Pellinore explains the details of his quest to the Wart, who listens attentively.

The Wart spends the night in the Forest Sauvage; the next day, he wanders until he stumbles upon Merlyn's cottage. The old magician introduces himself to the Wart, offers him breakfast, and tells the Wart that he will serve as his tutor. He and the Wart return to Sir Ector's castle, where Merlyn offers a display of his magical powers. After a month passes, Merlyn begins tutoring the Wart: His first lesson consists of turning him into a perch.

Commentary

The novel's epigraph serves as an invitation to the reader from T. H. White ("you and I") to enter a world of magic. "Gramarye" is an archaic word meaning "magic," and "Merlyn's Isle of Gramarye" refers not to the England of history, but of legend. Although the novel's style is often humorous and anachronistic, the characters are part of an old narrative and mythological tradition. The epigraph suggests to the reader that the novel's setting "is not any common earth" (one bound by the laws of physics as found in "realistic" fiction), but instead a place where uncommon occurrences and random moments of magic are the norm. Thus, the world of *The Sword in the Stone* is one where characters react in believable and understandable ways to unbelievable and fantastic events. For example, when the Wart is transformed into different animals, he feels all the emotions a reader would expect a person to feel upon becoming a fish, hawk, or badger—but the very impossibility of such transformations occurring is never questioned by any of the characters. Magic is as much of an accepted part of the characters' lives as gravity is of our own.

The novel begins with a description of the Wart and Kay's schedule of lessons, the sound of which reinforces its dryness and sterility: "On Mondays, Wednesdays and Fridays it was Court Hand and Summulae Logicales, while the rest of the week it was the Organon, Repetition, and Astrology." White begins the novel with this sentence to hint at the book's most important theme: the qualities of a good education and the means by which it is acquired. Throughout the novel, the Wart will learn lessons about humanity, although not from books, astrolabes, or the "Summulae Logicales." Destined to rule all of England, the Wart must learn about people, politics, and power before the title of "Once and Future King" can be conferred upon him. Because the reader knows that the Wart will eventually become King Arthur, White offers an array of characters and situations that allow the reader to see the different ways the boy acquires the qualities he needs to act as a loyal and responsible king. In short, much of White's novel is concerned with leadership and how a naive boy who knows little of the practical, political world becomes more knowledgeable about it, all without his even realizing that such an education is taking place.

Style & Language

Sir Ector's earnest but misguided desire for the boys to become "eddicated" is gently mocked by the narrator. For example, Sir Ector feels that true education resides in learning "Latin and stuff" as well as practical techniques for governing a household. However, Sir Ector is not a very good teacher, since he "shouts commands" at the servants making hay until he is "purple in the face." He also impedes the assistants' progress in doing so, while "stamping and perspiring" out of anger. Clearly, he is not destined to be the Wart's teacher, as one may expect a father figure to be. Sir Ector's past attempt at hiring a tutor resulted in a governess who physically punished the boys and who, the boys learn, had spent some time in a "lunatic hospital." The Wart will require an education—not a rustic's "eddication"—if he is to become King. Of course, the Wart has no idea of his future greatness and, like many children, would rather play than be tutored.

While introducing this theme, White simultaneously establishes the rivalry between the Wart and Kay. The Wart's name suggests his diminutive size and status in Sir Ector's household, as well as the way he is treated and viewed by Kay, who is two years older. Kay is "too dignified to have a nickname" and prides himself on knowing everything about horsemanship, jousting, and chivalry. Kay reminds the Wart that he (Kay) is Sir Ector's "proper son" and that this affords him the right to bark orders at his younger brother. Kay is conscious of what he sees as his status and place in society, disregarding Hob's advice on hawking because he is "only a villein" and hating the making of hay (a servant's duty). Kay is not, however, skilled at hawking (he loses Cully in a tree) or haying (he stands on the edges of the bundles he attempts to lift). Note that White illustrates Kay's pride while also demonstrating the effects of not accepting the advice of others.

Character Insight

While Kay is child*ish*, the Wart is child*like* in his naiveté and tendency to be easily impressed; according to the narrator, the Wart is "a born follower [and] hero-worshipper." Throughout the first five chapters, White emphasizes this aspect of the Wart's personality. For example, when the Wart first meets King Pellinore (on the trail of the Questing Beast), he thinks that Pellinore is the epitome of chivalry and heroism. The narrator describes Pellinore this way: "He was mounted on an enormous white horse that stood rapt as its master, and he carried in his right hand, with its butt resting on the stirrup, a high, smooth, jousting lance, which stood up among the tree stumps, higher and higher, till it was outlined against the velvet sky. All was moonlight, all silver, too beautiful to describe."

Even in his doubts over whether or not King Pellinore is a ghost (another boyish concern), the Wart decides that "even if it were a ghost, it would be the ghost of a knight, and knights were bound by their vows to help people in distress." The Wart's ideas about perfect practitioners of chivalry are straight out of folklore and legend—which he sees as fact. He is so rapt by King Pellinore's heroic status that he becomes more concerned with consoling the dejected man than finding his way back to Sir Ector.

The reader, however, views King Pellinore in a slightly different way: The King is likable and interesting, but he is also a bumbling parody of true knighthood. He struggles with his visor, calls his search for the Beast Glatisant "boring," and is more interested in the prospect of his own feather bed at Sir Ector's castle than fulfilling the demands of his quest. When he becomes entangled in his hound's leash and disappears into the forest yelling "Yoicks," the reader views him as an example of "education in reverse." Because the Wart is to become the greatest practitioner of questing and chivalry, White has him first see an example of what chivalry is not.

The Wart then meets his true tutor and mentor in Merlyn, whose cottage he discovers in a clearing. Although Merlyn, like King Pellinore, is introduced as a comic figure struggling with a water bucket and covered with bird droppings, he possesses a wisdom not found anywhere else in the novel. His physical description marks him as a traditional wizard of legend, complete with conical cap, zodiac-embroidered gown, long white beard, and magic wand. White also endows him, however, with the unusual malady of having to live backward through time; like the author of a novel or a supreme deity, Merlyn possesses a wisdom in the present that could otherwise only be acquired by seeing into the future. In other words, while humans progress forward in time, Merlyn was "born at the wrong end of time" and therefore regresses through time, carrying into the present all of his knowledge of the future. Merlyn compares his predicament to trying to write in a mirror, and therefore has the Wart try to write a "W" while looking into one. The fact that the Wart's "W" comes out as an "M" suggests the strange relationship between the boy and the wizard: The Wart is a young and inexperienced squire while Merlyn, an old, wise scholar, is his opposite (as a "W" is, *visually*, the opposite of "M"). With his "enormous meerschaum pipe," an allusion by White to another great literary genius, Sherlock Holmes, Merlyn will prove to be the source of all the Wart's future knowledge and wisdom.

The decor of Merlyn's cottage also suggests his upcoming role in the Wart's life. Crammed with books, examples of taxidermy, animated cutlery, and a talking owl named Archimedes, this setting resembles a university in miniature and reinforces Merlyn's importance to the Wart's education. Before they return to Sir Ector's, Merlyn teaches the Wart how to properly address Archimedes—the first of his many lessons. (The Wart's blunder of addressing Archimedes as "Archie" reveals, to the owl, his "ignorance.") When the Wart states, "Would you mind if

I ask you a question," Merlyn replies, "It is what I am for," demonstrating his idea of what a good teacher should be: One who attempts to provide answers for the willing student, although such answers are, throughout the novel, often given indirectly. In future chapters, Merlyn refrains from direct instruction and instead has the Wart *experience* the lessons that will make him ready to rule. The Wart's excitement at the prospect of Merlyn becoming his tutor is revealed in his exclamation, "I must have been on a Quest!" What the Wart does not realize, however, is that his "quest" is only beginning and will be more difficult and important than the comic one attempted by King Pellinore.

Unlike the Wart (and the reader), Sir Ector initially doubts Merlyn's ability to educate the Wart. When he requests some "testimonials" to Merlyn's abilities, he is given some tablets signed by Aristotle, a parchment signed by Hecate, and "some typewritten duplicates signed by the Master of Trinity." All three figures are ones associated with education: Aristotle was a Greek philosopher noted for his *Poetics* and books on reasoning, Hecate was (in Greek mythology) the Queen of witchcraft, and the Master of Trinity is the president of Trinity College, Oxford. Again, White stresses (in a humorous fashion) the importance of Merlyn's role. When Sir Ector further questions the magician's powers as a tutor, Merlyn changes the landscape and weather, removing any skepticism about his ability to "eddicate" the Wart from Sir Ector's mind. Here, Merlyn also demonstrates his personable side: When Kay is reproached by Merlyn for insulting the Wart—and feels guilty for doing so—Merlyn creates a little silver hunting-knife for him to suggest that he has "learned his lesson."

Theme

The Wart's first "formal" lesson from Merlyn occurs in Chapter 5, although the Wart does not realize that he is being taught—marking Merlyn as an excellent teacher who can, like the magician he certainly is, literally and figuratively "trick" a student into enjoying his education. The Wart still identifies learning with "stuffy classrooms" and is pleasantly surprised when Merlyn allows him to be transformed into a perch. His transformation into a fish is the first of many such transformations in the novel and it is important for a reader to understand why Merlyn adopts this particular teaching technique for the boy who, as Merlyn knows, will eventually become King. Because a King is supposed to represent all of his subjects in battle, diplomacy, and politics, Merlyn has the Wart meet many different kinds of people—all of which, however, are found in the different types of animals into which he is transformed. Only after being exposed to a variety of personalities, leaders, and followers will the Wart be ready.

When he first becomes a fish, the Wart has difficulty manipulating his fins and swimming in a straight line, and like the frightened boy that he is, he asks Merlyn to accompany him. Merlyn agrees, but not before explaining to the Wart why he will only accompany him on this one adventure: "Education is experience, and the essence of experience is self-reliance." With this remark, White suggests to the reader Merlyn's methods and goals as a teacher. Although a teacher should be able to answer any of his student's questions (as Merlyn suggests with his remark about "what he is for"), he should ultimately guide his student's education, rather than "spoon feed" him easy solutions to difficult problems. After Merlyn transforms himself into a tench (or carp) and shows the Wart how to stay level and live in "two planes, not one," the Wart must realign his perceptions and see the world from a different point-of-view to accommodate his new situation—something that any leader must be able to do when faced with a crisis. White's description of the Wart seeing the water's spectrum being separated into seven parts accentuates this idea: To truly become educated, one must be able to apprehend the world in a way to which he was previously unaccustomed. When the Merlyn attempts to correct the Wart's zigzagging by telling him, "You swim like a boy," he, too, is suggesting this same idea. A passing swan, who informs the Wart that it is not "deformed" as the Wart assumed it was, also causes the Wart to reconsider his past assumptions about life in the moat and people very different from himself.

Theme

The Wart's final lesson as a fish occurs when he meets Mr. P., the King of the Moat. Like King Pellinore, who suggests to the Wart what chivalry is by illustrating its obverse, Mr. P. indirectly teaches the Wart about good leadership tactics by showing him the effects of despotic rule on an individual long accustomed to enforcing it. White describes Mr. P.'s face as "ravaged by all the passions of an absolute monarch— by cruelty, sorrow, age, pride, selfishness, loneliness and thoughts too strong for individual brains." His "vast ironic mouth" is fixed in a permanent frown, and he offers the Wart a philosophy as pitiless and ruthless as his physical appearance suggests: "There is only power. Power is of the individual mind, but the mind's power is not enough. Power of the body decides everything in the end, and only Might is Right." Although he does not know it, the Wart is meeting this tyrant so that he can learn about a style of governing that he will do better to avoid. Because Mr. P. lives only for brute, physical power, he has become an uncaring, cold, and "inhuman" ruler. Indeed, he is so committed to power that he warns the Wart to leave before he attacks and eats him. If the boyish Wart is to become the chivalric King Arthur, he must understand what absolute power can do to a leader. His education, at the hands of Merlyn, has begun.

Glossary

(Here and in the following sections, difficult words and phrases are explained.)

Chapter 1

Summulae Logicales a treatise on logic by Pope John XXI, written in the thirteenth century.

Organon the title of Aristotle's (384–322 BC) writings on logic and thought.

tilting the sport of jousting, whereby two riders attempted to unhorse each other by charging at each other and hitting their opponents with lances.

the mort the note sounded on a hunting horn when the quarry is killed.

the undoing in hunting, the removal of one's arrows from the prey.

port a strong, sweet wine from Portugal.

Metheglyn a spiced or medicated kind of mead (a liquor made from fermented honey and water).

Hic, Haec, Hoc a joke by Sir Ector, who is pretending to offer the declension (or breakup of verb tenses) for his drunken hiccup.

pike a type of freshwater bony fish.

wattle and daub interlaced twigs and rods, plastered with mud or clay to make walls or roofs.

the cows were on their gad The cows were wandering aimlessly.

rick a stack of hay.

jerkins a short, closefitting jacket, often sleeveless, or a vest.

goshawk a large, swift, powerful hawk with short wings and a long, rounded tail.

mews cages for hawks.

tack gear; equipment.

cardamom a spice from the seeds of various East Indian plants.

jesses straps for fastening around a falcon's leg, with a ring at one end for attaching a leash.

merlins small European or North American falcons with a striped, brownish-red breast.

tiercels male hawks.

just been taken up from hacking If a hawk is "in hacking," he is not yet allowed to hunt food for itself.

peregrine a kind of falcon often used for hawking.

kestrel a small, reddish-gray falcon, noted for its ability to hover in the air with its head to the wind.

mutes here, feces.

austringers people who train and fly hawks.

deep in the moult a hawk at a stage of advanced moulting, or shedding its feathers.

conies rabbits.

villein any of a class of feudal serfs who by the thirteenth century had become freemen in their legal relations to all except their lord, to whom they remained subject as slaves.

Chapter 2

yarak a state of prime fitness in a hawk.

fewmets the droppings of the prey, used by the hunter to track it.

libbard a mispronunciation of "leopard."

brachet a hunting dog.

Chapter 3

tippet a scarf-like garment of fur, wool, etc. for the neck and shoulders, hanging down in front; historically worn by judges or religious officials.

cabalistic pertaining to signs and symbols of secret societies or factions.

lignum vitae Latin for "wood of life;" a type of tree used to make various medicines.

corkindrill a mythological beast.

phoenix a mythological bird that bursts into flame and then rises from its own ashes.

oleander a poisonous evergreen shrub.

astrolabe an instrument used to find the altitudes of stars.

satsuma a variety of Japanese pottery.

cloisonne pottery and china in which colored enamels are kept separate by thin metal strips.

pismires ants.

cigarette cards trading cards that used to be given out in cigarette packs.

truncheon a short, thick club used by policemen.

Chapter 4

greaves pieces of armor that cover the shins.

Aristotle (384–322 BC) Greek philosopher and pupil of Plato, noted for works on logic, metaphysics, ethics, politics, and so on.

Hecate a goddess of the moon, earth, and underground realm of the dead, later regarded as the goddess of sorcery and witchcraft.

Master of Trinity Dean of Trinity College, Oxford.

Cromwell Oliver Cromwell (1599–1658), British Puritan general and Lord Protector of England from 1653–58.

stoat a kind of ermine, or weasel, whose fur is often used for coats and robes.

Chapter 5

vespers the sixth of the seven canonical hours, or the service for it occurring in the late afternoon or early evening.

barbican a defensive tower or similar fortification at a gate or bridge leading into a town or castle.

bartizans a small, overhanging turret on a tower or a castle.

portcullis a heavy iron grating suspended by chains and lowered between grooves to bar the gateway of a castle or fortified town.

tracery stone ornamental open-work found in castle windows.

bosses ornamental projecting pieces, as at the intersection of the ribs of an arched roof.

the Marches the borderlands of England and Scotland.

byres cow barns.

M.F.H. Master of Foxhounds.

Agincourt a village in Northern France where King Henry V defeated the French in 1415.

alaunts, gaze-hounds, lymers and **braches** different kinds of hounds.

purlieus regions.

Chapters 6 and 7

Summary

The Wart and Kay practice their archery by playing a game called Rovers. Kay kills his first rabbit; after the boys skin and gut it, the Wart shoots an arrow into the air, which is snatched in mid-flight by a crow. Kay contends that the crow was really a witch.

On a day toward the end of the summer, as the Wart sits near the tilting-yard and watches Kay practice his skills, the Wart confides to Merlyn his desire to be a knight, as Kay will surely become. Merlyn agrees to let the Wart see some real battle on a tilting field, and casts a spell that transports him and the Wart to the Forest Sauvage, where they watch King Pellinore and Sir Grummore Grummursum joust. Eventually, the two combatants are knocked unconscious when they each charge at the other, miss, and then ram their heads into the trunks of trees. Merlyn then casts another spell that transports him and the Wart back to the tilting ground.

Commentary

Kay's description of the arrow-stealing crow as a "witch" is somewhat accurate. In Chapter 11, the boys will see the crow sitting on top of the castle of The Oldest Ones of All, allowing the reader to infer that the crow is actually an animal-spirit, that serves the sorceress Morgan Le Fay, who is keeping watch over the Wart and Kay. Later in the novel, they will encounter her face-to-face during their adventures with Robin Wood.

More important in these two chapters is the joust between King Pellinore and Sir Grummore, which reveals different attitudes toward jousting (and proving one's heroism through it). White begins Chapter 7 by offering his reader an extensive survey of jousting traditions, equipment, and practices. After treating such topics as how a lance should be held, the proper length of a lance, and where an enemy should be hit with one, the narrator concludes, "It would take too long to go into all the interesting details of proper tilting which the boys had to learn, for in those days, you had to be a master of your craft from the bottom upward." In this light, tilting is a noble sport that requires great discipline, courage, and expertise.

This attitude is shared by the Wart with regard to the "craft" of tilting, because, as he views it, the sport is connected to knighthood and he desperately wants to be a knight. When asked by Merlyn why he is "grieving" while watching Kay practice his tilting, the Wart almost breaks out in tears and explains, "I shall not be a knight because I am not a proper son of Sir Ector's. They shall knight Kay, and I shall be his squire." When asked, by Merlyn, to elaborate on this complaint, .the Wart says that if he was born with a "proper father and mother," he would have become a "knight-errant" with a "splendid suit of armor and dozens of spears and a black horse standing eighteen hands." He also remarks that he would have called himself "The Black Knight," challenged random knights in a wood for the right to pass him, and only begrudgingly married—because he would need a "lady-love" who would allow him to wear her favor in his helm as he did "deeds in her honor." Clearly, the Wart has been hypnotized by legends and lore; his ideas about knights and chivalry are worn and cliched. Again, White stresses the Wart's naiveté and boyishness; his yearning for knighthood is reminiscent of the young Mark Twain's desire to become a riverboat captain

White uses Merlyn to offer the reader the reader an attitude about knighthood that directly opposes the Wart's. At the very beginning of Chapter 7, Merlyn complains that "people seemed to think you were an educated man if you could knock a man off a horse." He gives Sir Ector, an "old tilting blue," rheumatism to keep him from bragging about his days of glory on the tilting field; later, he describes knights as "brainless unicorns swaggering about" and "calling themselves educated because they can push each other off a horse with a bit of stick." To Merlyn, tilting is only a game (and a silly one, at that), adopted by the English because of the "games-mad" Norman aristocracy. The degree to which Merlyn values education is established earlier in the novel, and White employs the magician here to dispel some of the clichés believed by the Wart and, possibly, by some readers of the novel.

However, a reader may ask why Merlyn, after his disparaging remarks about jousts, would then transport the Wart to the scene of one. The answer becomes obvious when the reader meets the two combatants: Sir Grummore, the tippling knight who banters with Sir Ector in Chapter 1, and King Pellinore, the bumbling hunter of the Questing Beast met in Chapter 2. Merlyn wants the Wart to see a joust in its most full, ridiculous splendor. By seeing two knights whose practice of jousting falls far short of the Wart's grandiose ideals, Merlyn will (he hopes) be able to continue the Wart's education and teach him about the difference between boyish fantasy and adult realities.

Style &
Language

Throughout the joust, the participants repeatedly attempt to follow a scripted formula that is as cliched as the Wart's ideas about himself as "The Black Knight." Both men *want* to appear graceful and meet the universally accepted standards for chivalric behavior found in legend, but their inadequacies continually undermine their attempts. One method used by White to suggest the men's shortcomings is his stressing the physical clumsiness of the match. For example, when donning his armor, Pellinore is not graceful (like those knights seen in films) but clumsy: He had "set on the wrong thread when getting up in a hurry that morning" and, as a result, requires "quite a feat of engineering" to get his armor ready for battle. Later, the reader learns that the knights' movements are "so hampered by his burden of iron" that they appear to be fighting in "slow motion"; the notion of the swashbuckling hero falls flat in light of this description. When they first make contact, Pellinore and Grummore are compared to "a motor omnibus in collision with a smithy"; after they fall, "it took them so long to get up" that "every stage of the contest could be marked and pondered." During the second stage, Grummore "stumped off" to one end of the field, while Pellinore "plodded off" to the other, because "even walking was complicated." When they clash for the second time, the noise is compared to a "shipwreck and great bells tolling." Pellinore then gets up but cannot find Sir Grummore; when he eventually does, Pellinore pushes Sir Grummore down, instead of smiting him with a perfect blow. During their final encounter, they charge each other and miss their targets, but "the momentum of their armor was too great for them to stop until they had passed each other handsomely" and they eventually have to resort to "waving their arms like windmills" in an effort to stop. The final moment of physical comedy occurs when both men run headfirst into trees and, with "a last melodious clang," fall "prostrate on the fatal sward." Clearly, Pellinore and Grummore resemble second-rate acrobats and clowns more than the majestic fighters that the Wart expects all such men to be. Pellinore's complaint to

Grummore, "Oh, come on . . . You know you have to yield when your helm is off," suggests the degree to which the men wholeheartedly accept the conventions of storybook chivalry.

Another way that White satirizes the Wart's naive view of combat is his making the fighters linguistically clumsy as well: The language used by the combatants is an attempt to seem serious and earnest but sounds melodramatic and silly. For example, Merlyn immediately begins mocking the entire scene by saying "Hail" to King Pellinore three different times; each time, Pellinore responds with his own "Hail" because he is anxious to "make a good impression." After Sir Grummore's refusal to tell Pellinore his name (which Pellinore obviously knows yet asks about because doing so is part of the formula), Pellinore states that "no knight ne dreadeth for to speak his name openly, but for some reason of shame." Grummore's reply is similar in style: "Be that as it may, I choose that thou shalt not know my name as at this time, for no askin'." Both men are attempting to sound "regal" through the use of words such as "dreadeth" and "thou," and, of course, their highly artificial speech sounds phony (and funny) to the reader. The obviousness of their charade is highlighted when, during the same exchange, Grummore corrects one of Pellinore's lines from "You must stay and joust with me" to "Thou shalt stay and joust with me." This kind of talk continues throughout the match, with phrases such as "Defend thee" and Yield thee, recreant" contrasting the physical buffoonery of their speakers. Eventually, even Pellinore and Grummore "forget their lines" when they begin childishly bickering over whether Pellinore said, "Pax": Their repetitions of "Yes, you did" and "No, you didn't" highlights the reader's understanding of just how wide the gulf is between the knights' high ideals and actual behavior.

To the Wart, however, Pellinore and Grummore are nothing less than glorious: When the match finally begins, the Wart yells, "They're off" and is described as "holding his breath with excitement." As the two begin fighting, he asks Merlyn if he thinks they will "kill each other," to which the wizard replies, "Dangerous sport." This pattern of an earnest remark by the Wart, followed by an ironic understatement from Merlyn, continues throughout the joust and, as with the Wart's meeting Pellinore in Chapter 2, serves to illustrate the Wart's completely boyish attitude toward what is obviously (to both Merlyn and the reader) a ridiculous spectacle. At one point, the Wart covers his eyes and asks Merlyn if it is "safe to look"; he replies, "Quite safe," because "It will take them some time to get back in position." The

Wart, however, never senses the irony of Merlyn's responses, and continues to reveal his childlike attitude toward the contest. For example, after Pellinore is hit by Grummore, the Wart calls him, "Poor King," and says, "I wish he would not hit him so"; when Pellinore pushes his opponent after saying "Pax," the Wart exclaims, "What a cheat! I would not have thought it of him." After the fighters' final "clang," the Wart asks Merlyn if they should help them, to which the wizard remarks, "We could pour water on their heads . . . But I don't suppose they would thank us for making their armour rusty." Merlyn sees the folly of thinking that one's skill at tilting is indicative of one's worth and is indirectly trying to make the Wart see it, too. However, when the match is over, the Wart asks Merlyn if Pellinore will be able to sleep in one of Grummore's feather beds and says that doing so would be "nice" for the King, "even if he was stunned." The boy's devotion to the theory of knighthood—rather than its practice—is both charming and sentimental, but if he is ever to face real, practical matters of leadership, such youthful ideals will need to be readjusted.

Glossary

Chapter 6

hummocks low, rounded hills.

coney a rabbit.

portent a supernatural warning or hint of danger.

Chapter 7

tilting jousting.

quintain an object supported by a crosspiece on a post, used by knights as a target in tilting.

saracen an Arab or Muslim of the time of the Crusades.

bosh foolishness.

Norman pertaining to the victors of the Norman Invasion of England (1066); the British kings from William the Conqueror (ruled 1066–1087) to Stephen (ruled 1135–1154) were Norman kings.

a knight errant a knight who wanders in search of adventure.

panoply a complete suit of armor.

from crupper to poll from the horse's rear to its head.

twenty-two stone 308 pounds (a British "stone" equals 14 pounds).

sward grass-covered soil.

nob the head.

Pax a "kiss of peace" in which the combatant surrenders to his opponent.

Chapter 8

Summary

Near the end of August, the Wart finds himself an outcast from his own castle: Ector, Kay, the Nurse, Hob, the sergeant, and even the Dog Boy all complain of having no time for him. Dejected, he visits Merlyn, who is knitting a nightcap. After the Wart pleads with him, Merlyn agrees to turn the Wart into a hawk. Merlyn carries the Wart (as a hawk) to the mews; during the night, the Wart learns of the hawks' military-like life and passes a test of his courage, which earns his acceptance in their company.

Commentary

As in previous conversations, the one between Merlyn and the Wart at the beginning of the chapter reveals Merlyn's plans for the Wart's education. Merlyn explains that he will eventually turn the Wart into "everything in the world" for the sake of his education. In the same conversation, Merlyn states that "the way to learn" is "by listening to the experts." The wizard's allowing the Wart to become a hawk, therefore, is more than an act of kindness: Understanding the hawks will become another factor in the boy's expanding awareness of different ways of life.

Merlyn compares the mews to a "kind of Spartan military mess" and this description is proved true in a number of ways. The hawks place great emphasis on ancestry (the Wart is asked to name the "branch" of merlins from which he hails); decorum (Cully is routinely reprimanded for talking out of turn and using the word "damned"); and rank (the peregrine must be addressed as "Madam," Balan tells her that the Wart's family must be descended from a "cadet branch," and Cully suffers from the "constant strain" of having to live up to "his ladyship's standard"). The hawks are also compared to knights, standing "gravely in their plumed helmets, spurred and armed." Merlyn's reason for wanting the Wart to learn about this way of life lies in his desire for the Wart to see *real* honor and discipline, as opposed to the parody of these qualities witnessed in the tilting match between Pellinore and Grummore in

Chapter 7. Exposure to such a strident yet noble way of life cannot but help to make the Wart an honorable King when he is called to be.

However, the Wart, like any other cadet, must prove his worth to the assembly of soldiers. First, he must, in a very strict fashion, pass a test of his knowledge of the catechism, which he does (with the aid of Balan); his score of "ninety per cent" suggests that the Wart is in a unique type of classroom where more "eddication" is taking place. The entire catechism test is reminiscent of a soldier's having to know proper military procedures and rules. Next, he must be "sworn in" by a padre, much like all members of any military, including knights, take oaths to uphold their codes of behavior. The Wart's greatest test, in keeping with the military air of the mews, is one of physical courage: He must stand next to Cully (who threatens to attack him) for three rings of a bell. This frightens the Wart, but he decides that he must go "through with this ordeal to earn his education." Merlyn's plan to imbue the Wart with a sense of courage works in this case, because the Wart is more brave at this point than he has yet shown himself to be in the novel thus far. His passing the hawks' tests is celebrated in the singing of "patriotic" songs that reveal the values of those who uphold the code of the mews: The first song states, "Shame to the slothful and woe to the weak one," while the second praises the boy's bravery: "His birds and beasts / Supply our feasts, / And his feats our glorious chorus!"

Although the Wart is not viewed as "glorious" by the members of Ector's household, he has found true honor in the mews. As Balan remarks, "We shall have a regular king in that young candidate;" later in the Wart's coming-of-age, these words will prove more true than anyone—except Merlyn and the reader—expects.

Glossary

mews cages for hawks.

protista kingdom of organisms including bacteria and protozoa.

nigromant a magician.

Spartan military mess Sparta was a city in ancient Greece, famous for the strict discipline of its soldiers. A "mess" is a mess hall, where soldiers eat.

regulars common soldiers.

subaltern in the British military, holding an army commission below that of captain.

catechism a handbook of questions and answers for teaching the principles of a religion.

dree enduring, suffering.

Timor Mortis Conturbant Me Latin, "The fear of death disturbs me."

Timor Mortis Exultat Me Latin, "The fear of death overjoys me."

Chapters 9–12

Summary

The next morning, Kay reprimands the Wart for not returning last night. When the Wart will not reveal where he was, the boys have a fist-fight in which Kay suffers a bloody nose and the Wart receives a black eye. After Kay cries to the Wart about how he feels rejected by Merlyn, the Wart visits the magician and asks if he can transform him and Kay into snakes (or another animal). Merlyn refuses to transform Kay into anything, because he was "sent" only to work his magic on the Wart. However, Merlyn does tell the Wart that he and Kay will find an adventure if they walk along Hob's strip of barley until they "come to something."

After becoming friends again, the boys follow Merlyn's advice; eventually, they enter the Forest Sauvage and encounter Much and Little John, two of Robin Wood's sentries. (Little John explains that the name "Robin *Hood*" is incorrect.) They soon meet the legendary bandit himself, lying in the lap of Maid Marian, his wife. He tests the boys' skill at archery and explains to them that Friar Tuck (one of their companions) and the Dog Boy (one of Ector's servants) have been kidnapped by The Oldest Ones of All: A race of fairies whose Queen, Morgan Le Fay, is "one of the worst of them." After hearing this news, the boys agree to help Robin storm the Castle Chariot and save the captives.

The plan to raid the Castle Chariot is reviewed in detail: Robin explains that only boys and girls can enter the castle and that it is guarded by a griffin—a beast that is part falcon, lion, and serpent. The boys are also warned about the effects of iron on the fairies (it will lessen their powers and thus make them aware that the boys are near) and to not eat anything they see inside the castle, however tempting it may look. The boys join Robin's band of one hundred men and make their way to the Castle Chariot; they eventually find the griffin, sneak by it, and reach the castle, which is made entirely of food. (They also see the crow from Chapter 6 perched atop it.) Kay and the Wart enter the castle, alert Morgan Le Fay with their iron knives, and charge her; the castle then collapses and disappears, freeing the captives. A battle with the griffin ensues and Kay rescues the Wart by killing it as it attacks his younger brother. Finally, after saying goodbye to Robin and his men, the boys return—as heroes—to the Castle of the Forest Sauvage. Chapter 12 ends with Wat and the Dog Boy reunited as friends.

Commentary

The parable told by Merlyn at the beginning of Chapter 9 serves as his explanation of why he can tutor only the Wart and also analogously depicts the relationship between the wizard and his tutor. In the parable, Elijah (a Biblical prophet) and Rabbi Jachanan are traveling and stay at a poor man's home and then in the cowshed of a rich merchant. According to Merlyn, the Rabbi Jachanan was incensed at what he saw as the prophet's inappropriate degree of thankfulness to the two hosts. Elijah offered no sympathy for the poor man when he awoke to find his only cow dead, but sent for a mason to repair a crumbling wall on the merchant's property. Elijah then instructed his companion on his methods: Although it was decreed that the poor man's wife was to die that night, God spared her (for her husband's kindness) and took the cow instead. Similarly, although the miser could have certainly afforded to hire his own mason, Elijah sent one immediately in order to prevent the miser from discovering a chest of gold that, if discovered, would have certainly excited his avarice. Thus, the parable's theme is the all-knowingness of God—Elijah's lesson to the Rabbi is, "Say not therefore to the Lord: What doest thou? But say in thy heart: Must not the Lord of all the earth do right?" As the Rabbi spoke without understanding and needed to be taught by Elijah, so the Wart, in his ignorance, asks Merlyn to transform Kay into an animal and needs to be taught by his mentor; as Merlyn says, "It is unfair," but the situation is also ordained by God. Like his counterpart in the parable, the Wart is unaware that there are forces greater than himself at work in determining the fates of those around him. Although Merlyn is "sorry" that the Wart "should be the only one to get [his] extra tuition," he "was only sent for that." Kingship is predetermined, and this is one of the first moments in the novel in which White intimates that the book's entire action, from the very beginning, has been "decreed" in order to bring the Wart to the jousting tournament in London, where he will discover his role as "once and future King."

Until that time, however, the Wart will need to content himself with his faith in Merlyn, a faith that is always rewarded. His desire for an adventure that he can share with Kay results in another lesson in a different kind of "classroom." Merlyn's decision to have the Wart meet Robin Wood is very much like his making the boy spend time in the mews. He wants the Wart to observe admirable and heroic qualities in others so that he will have the memory of sufficient role models to guide is behavior once he is King. Robin Hood is not an Arthurian character *per se*, but one found in ballads of the later Middle Ages; however, the fun (and irony) of these chapters lies in the fact that they describe one legendary character meeting another—although one of the two does not know of his future legendary status. As one of the Wart's many teachers, Robin is invaluable: He is physically agile, tender (singing duets with Maid Marian), and a steadfast leader of men who resists oppression and tyranny (his soldiers are compared to those "of the resistance in later occupations"). Also, note that Maid Marian is another of the Wart's teachers, instructing him in the best ways to walk through a virgin forest without making any noise.

The core of the Wart's adventure with Robin Wood is his rescue of Friar Tuck and the Dog Boy from the Oldest Ones of All. White could have invented any sort of test in which the Wart could learn about courage, but a careful reader will note that White ascribes to the fairies (and their Queen, Morgan Le Fay) a quality that a future leader should definitely not possess: gluttony. One of the fairies' oldest poems describes a castle made out of "thin pressed cheese," "a bacon house," and "pillars of marvelous pork," and when the boys face Morgan Le Fay, she is not the vixen that she sometimes appears to be in legend, but instead is a "fat" and "dowdy" woman lying on a bed of "glorious lard." While the gluttony depicted here is the literal gorging of food, figurative gluttony must also be avoided lest a leader begin to resemble Mr. P. (the perch who gorges on power in Chapter 5) or, to a lesser degree, Kay (who, at the end of the adventure, will "gorge" on the glory of killing the griffin). Moderation, not extremity, is one key to a successful reign. Robin epitomizes discipline (he leads a hundred men and makes them recite their plans twice to be sure that they are understood); it is therefore fitting that his (and the Wart's) enemies here should be ones associated with a lack of discipline. The fairies are Robin Wood's enemies philosophically as well as physically, and Merlyn (who, like Elijah, knows more than his pupil) wants their gluttony to appear distasteful to the future King.

The outcome of the adventure reveals a fundamental difference between the Wart and Kay and—on a bigger scale—two ways of regarding one's victory in battle. To Kay, victory is a means by which glory is obtained: He boasts that he "shot dozens" of griffins and undoubtedly revels in his father's decision to have the griffin's head mounted, as a trophy, with "KAY'S FIRST GRIFFIN" written on a card underneath it. To the Wart, however, victory is an opportunity to use one's power for the good of others. When asked by Robin to name any reward for his courage, the Wart asks to take Wat (the mad wanderer of the forest) to Merlyn so that he could get his "wits" restored with the wizard's help. Kay thinks of himself while the Wart is selfless: Even at Sir Ector's, his only desire is to see that Wat reaches Merlyn's study. Kay's energies are focused inward and work for the good of his own reputation; the Wart's energies are focused outward on assisting others. His compassion will eventually be one of the reasons for his beloved stature as King Arthur.

Glossary

Chapter 9

helot one of a class of serfs in ancient Sparta.

Erasmus Erasmus Desiderius (about 1466–1536), Dutch humanist, scholar, and theologian.

Chapter 10

brambles and bindweed and honeysuckle and convolvulus and teazles and the stuff which country people call sweethearts various types of wild plants.

fritillaries butterflies, usually having brownish wings with silver spots on the undersides.

Saxons a tribe of Germanic warriors who (with the Angles, another Germanic tribe) invaded parts of Britain in the 5th and 6th centuries; here, the word is used by Robin Wood to denote those British people who resisted the Norman invasion of 1066.

Gaels the race of Gaelic-speaking Celts, displaced by the Anglo-Saxon invasions in the 5th and 6th centuries.

Circe the ancient Greek goddess of witchcraft; in *The Odyssey*, she turns unwitting sailors into swine.

Chapter 11

griffin a mythical monster with the body and hind legs of a lion and the head, wings, and claws of an eagle.

Weyve a female outlaw.

stridulation the sound made by a grasshopper.

the book of Sir John de Mandeville (1371) a famous book of travels that also describes fantastic people and creatures that the author claims to have seen in Africa and the Orient.

a wattling of tripe a roof made of tripe, or cow's stomach.

chitterlings the small intestines of pigs, used for food, usually fried in deep fat.

Chapter 12

mnemonic a short phrase or sentence used to jog one's memory, such as Every Good Boy Does Fine to recall the five notes (E, G, B, D, F) on the musical scale.

assonances rhymes ("what" and "wat").

Chapter 13

Summary

Since his return from his adventure three days earlier, the Wart has been confined to his bed to rest to regain his strength. Naturally, he is bored; his only amusement is the set of ant-nests that he took from Merlyn's cottage. Looking at the ants gives the Wart the idea to ask Merlyn transform him into one, and the wizard reluctantly agrees.

As an ant, the Wart does not fit in with the collective spirit of the colony; however, he does his best to perform his "antly" duties. He learns about the two basic utterances in the ants' language ("done" and "not done") and tries to complete his job as a member of the mash squad: A group of ants who fill their crops with the scrapings of seeds and then allow other ants to feed directly from their mouths. Eventually, an ant from a rival nest approaches the Wart's colony and is murdered—a war ensues. Merlyn rescues the Wart and transforms him back into a boy before the two ant armies engage in battle.

Commentary

Theme

As Mr. P. taught the Wart about tyranny and the hawks taught him about military honor, the ants introduce the Wart to a world of intense collectivism or communism, which reveals to him the horrors of this political philosophy. In a world where everyone (except the leader) is equal, life becomes incredibly monotonous and static; examples of these qualities in the ants' lives abound in this chapter. For example, the "wireless broadcast" received by the Wart's antennae begins to "make him feel sick" after an hour of its repetitions. None of the ants have names (which might suggest personalities), but numbers (the Wart's is 42436/WD). All ants speak in the same "dead" and "impersonal" voice and the narrator states, very bluntly, that "Novelties did not happen to them." Their conversations, like their lives, are the same day after day.

One way in which the ants are controlled by their leader without their ever considering their own situation is through their language, which reduces most words and phrases into either "done" or "not done."

As in George Orwell's *1984*, during which the totalitarian government employs a language called Newspeak that prohibits comparative phrases (and thus, the populace's comparing its own government to that of other nations), the ants' inability to speak of such things as "happiness," "freedom," "liking," or any of their opposites prevents them from ever realizing that these things do, in fact, exist. Put more simply, if a word does not exist for a thing, the thing cannot be pondered—and, if it cannot be pondered, it will never arise as a consideration in anyone's life. (This is why tyrants, throughout history, have burned books that articulated ideas contrary to their own political agendas.) Because "done" and "not done" apply to "all questions of value," the ants' thinking lacks the sophistication needed to consider complicated political questions. In fact, the very idea of asking questions is alien to the ants—"life was not questionable: it was dictated." If an act (or ant) serves the colony, it is "done" because life here is a matter of "duty," not free will.

When the Wart attempts to make sense of how any thinking creatures could live under such conditions, he (like a dissident in a communist country) is attacked for his temerity. Upon being asked what he is doing by a roving worker, the Wart replies, "I am not doing anything." Here, White is toying with the ambiguities of language and how these ambiguities vanish when the speakers strip the language of its subtleties. The Wart's reply is meant as a defense: He feels accused of wrongdoing, and uses the phrase "not doing anything" to mean "doing nothing wrong." To the inquiring ant, however, "not doing anything" *is* wrong in the *literal* sense of communism: A worker must, at all times, serve the community. This is why the ant reports that "There is an insane ant on square five"; decoding the ambiguities of language (even simple ones like this) requires a level of thinking that the ants do not possess. For the same reasons, the ant is unable to detect the Wart's sarcasm when he tells him, "I have fallen on my head and can't remember anything"; he reports that the "Not-Done ant has a black-out from falling of the nest." In a world where "EVERYTHING NOT FORBIDDEN IS COMPULSORY," language must not allow any room for free thought, which could, if encouraged, destroy the entire colony. The ants exist, like the Wart when he acts as a "dumbwaiter," only to serve.

The ants' reaction to death and war are equally static and unemotional. When the Wart sees two dead ants, they are described (from the Wart's point-of-view) as "curled up" and "did not seem to be either glad or sorry to be dead. They were there, like a couple of chairs." The ants are not affected by seeing the "cadavers" of their own kind, as seen when the new ant arrives to clear away (in a bumbling fashion) the corpses. The Wart, himself, would have also been a corpse, had Merlyn not given him the proper smell for the nest—like "done" and "not done" as words, the ants only smell "nest" and "not nest," and will kill any ant that proves to be an outsider. The logic they employ to justify their war is as unsophisticated as their language:

A. We are so numerous that we are starving.

B. Therefore we must encourage still larger families so as to become yet more numerous and starving.

C. When we are so numerous and starving as all that, obviously we shall have a right to take other people's stores of seed. Besides, we shall by then have a numerous and starving army.

Literary Device

White is parodying here the kind of thinking employed in the name of "just cause" for war. The cold and syllogistic "logic" attempted by the ants only serves to belie their selfishness and belligerence. They even resort to religious appeals (speaking of "Ant the Father") in order to justify their aggression. However, while this may seem shocking to the Wart (and the reader), the ants are never excited by the prospects of war: "They accepted them as matters of course" and as "Done." The Wart's depression resulting from "the dreary blank which replaced feeling," "the dearth of all but two values," and "the total monotony" teach him about the "wickedness" of a collective community, where a seemingly noble idea (work for the good of others) is employed to keep everyone working like robots and satisfy a leader's lust for war.

Glossary

Miss Edith Cavell (1865–1915); an English nurse executed by the Germans in World War I.

emmets ants.

Chapters 14–16

Summary

As autumn arrives, Sir Ector receives a letter from Uther Pendragon, the King of Gramarye, in which he is told of the King's plan to send Sir William Twyti, the royal huntsman, to the Forest Sauvage in order to kill two or three wild boars. Sir Ector is expected to provide food and lodging for Twyti (and his retinue), as well as salt the boar flesh to keep it fresh until Twyti's departure. Sir Ector is upset about the news (which he calls "a confounded piece of tyranny"), because he will have to turn his own hounds out of their kennels to lodge the royal ones, and make a number of similar accommodations. He consoles himself with the thought that perhaps Twyti and his men will be eaten in the forest by griffin.

That Christmas night, a tremendous feast is held in Sir Ector's castle to celebrate the arrival of Twyti. Sir Grummore, King Pellinore, Twyti, and an old man named Ralph Passelewe all sing rousing songs to the delight of the entire village. Sir Ector ends the feast with a set speech he has recited before and the singing of the national anthem.

The next day, the Wart wakes up very excited about the prospect of the hunt. After White describes the dangers and terrors of boar hunting, the hunt begins. Robin Wood arrives and Sir Ector nervously introduces him to Grummore and Pellinore. Grummore is charged by a boar and is hurt; eventually, the boar is trapped in a fallen tree and is killed by Robin. Twyti becomes tearful when he learns that Beaumont, one of his hounds, has had his back broken by the boar. Robin puts the dog out of his misery; to lighten the mood, White has Pellinore find the Questing Beast pining away for Pellinore, who promises to forsake Grummore's feather bed and resume his hunt for his "old beast" of a friend.

Commentary

The Wart is conspicuously absent from most of these chapters, allowing White to focus instead on the atmosphere and setting of the land that he will one day come to rule. White's nostalgia for a bygone, legendary, "merry England" is apparent throughout these chapters: feudalism, eating with one's fingers, and even the weather (which "behaved itself") are cast in the soft light of sentimentality, not unlike the way that many Americans think back on a mythical 1950s. Of course, the Middle Ages (and the 1950s) were not exactly the way they are portrayed in literature, but White is more interested in warming his readers' hearts than in offering them a realistic view of medieval life.

The boar hunt, for all of its excitement, is the most violent passage in the novel, and contrasts greatly with the merrymaking of Ector's feast the night before. Worth noting is the fact that Twyti, a professional hunter, is bored by his occupation and feels trapped in his role; without realizing so, he is very much like one of the ants in Chapter 13. His desire to hunt for hares (which, unlike boars, are harmless but difficult to catch) reveals his desire to break free from his royal duties.

Another contrast in the hunting scene occurs when the Wart spies tears on Twyti's face after he finds Beaumont with a broken back: "He stroked Beaumont's head and said, "Hark to Beaumont. Softly, Beaumont, mon amy. Oyez à Beaumont the valiant. Swef, le douce Beaumont, swef, swef." Beaumont licked his hand but could not wag his tail." Twyti's speaking in French and Beaumont's inability to wag his tail evoke a sense of pity from the reader; ironically, all the violence of the hunt is not as effective as this odd scene. (White's description of Robin's killing Beaumont is also sentimental, because he is not described as killing Beaumont but instead as allowing him to run free with Orion, the mythical hunter made famous in a constellation.) Even a man as accustomed to blood as is Twyti can reveal his fragility at the strangest moments.

While the reader feels real pity for Twyti and Beaumont, the "pity" evoked for Pellinore and the Questing Beast is infused with much more humor. The Questing Beast's illness is a result of her being ignored by Pellinore, and the former quester speaks to his old prey with language more appropriate to an old lover: "I didn't mean to leave you altogether!' and "Poor creature . . . It has pined away, positively pined away, just because there was nobody to take an interest in it" are two of Pellinore's outbursts as he caresses the Beast. The gravity of the previous scene highlights the comedy of this one, which recalls Chapter 7, in which the Wart witnessed the formulaic joust between Grummore and Pellinore; here, the Questing Beast is upset because Pellinore has abandoned the formula in which, together, they made a team. Resolving to forsake worldly comforts of feather beds in favor of the Questing Beast's "fewmets," Pellinore wholeheartedly returns to the formula of hunter and hunted that once gave his life so much meaning. He is as nostalgic for his old game of "hunt the Beast" as White is for merry England.

Glossary

Chapter 14

sowers planters.

bracken large, coarse, weedy ferns, occurring in meadows, woods, and especially wastelands.

feudal system the economic, political, and social system in medieval Europe, in which land, worked by serfs who were bound to it, was held by vassals in exchange for military and other services given to overlords.

beasts of venery animals pursued in hunting.

partisan a member of an organized civilian force fighting covertly to drive out occupying enemy troops; here, a term used to describe Robin Wood.

solar a private or upper chamber.

mullions slender, vertical dividing bars between the lights of windows, doors, and so on.

Chapter 15

Boxing Day the first weekday after Christmas, when gifts or "boxes" are given to employees, postmen, and so on.

mead an alcoholic liquor made of fermented honey and water.

morris dances old folk dances formerly common in England, especially on May Day, in which fancy costumes were worn, often those associated with characters in the Robin Hood legends.

sherries sack or malmsey wine two types of sweet wine.

"D'ye ken William Twyti?" "Do you recognize William Twyti?" spoken in a Northern English dialect.

Chapter 16

chine a cut of meat containing part of the backbone.

the richesses of martens, the bevies of roes, the cetes of badgers and the routs of wolves "richesses," "bevies," "cetes," and "routs" are all names for groups of the animals with which they are listed (as in "a school of fish").

Lord Baden-Powell British general (1857–1941), founder of Boy Scouts and Girl Guides.

baldrick a belt worn over one shoulder and across the chest to the hip, used to support a sword or horn.

falchion a medieval sword with a short, broad, slightly curved blade.

four long notes of the mort the song played on a hunting horn to announce the death of the prey.

Chapters 17–19

Summary

On an afternoon in the early spring, Merlyn announces to the Wart that he needs "another dose of education." The Wart asks to be transformed into a bird, but not a hawk, because he wants to learn to fly (as a hawk, he was confined to the mews). The Wart, Merlyn, and Archimedes begin discussing the language of birds and each of their favorites: The Wart votes for the rook, Archimedes for the pigeon, and Merlyn for the chaffinch. Merlyn offers his theory on the origin of birds' language, claiming that birds have grown to imitate their prey and the sounds of their surroundings. Kay, who enters after having killed a thrush with his crossbow, interrupts their discussion.

That night, Archimedes comes to the Wart and tells him to eat a mouse—which, oddly, the Wart does without any "nasty" feelings. The boy is then transformed into an owl and is taught to fly by Archimedes, who also lectures him on the gracefulness of the *plover* (another different breed of bird). Archimedes informs the Wart that Merlyn wants him to become a wild goose; the Wart then finds himself flying in the "enormous flatness" of the air. As one of approximately four hundred geese, the Wart learns of their music, traditions, and migratory rituals. Lyo-lyok, a female goose, befriends the Wart and becomes his temporary mentor. Eventually, the Wart and the other geese migrate across the North Sea. The Wart is then awakened, in his own bed, by Kay, who claims that the Wart was snoring "like a goose" all night.

Commentary

Theme

The discussion between the Wart, Merlyn, and Archimedes of their favorite birds is White's satirical look at social class and the relations between the sexes. While the Wart loves the rooks, Archimedes "loftily" reiterates the Wart's description of them as "mobs"—to the owl; rooks are lower-station birds who should be dismissed for the very frivolity that the Wart finds so appealing. Archimedes' love of the pigeon reveals his own values: He praises the "philosophical" nature of the bird and its complete sobriety. Merlyn's vote is more humorous, because he selects the chaffinch because they "have the sense to separate during the winter, so that all the males are in one flock and all the females in the other." Because of this separation, Merlyn explains that in "the winter months, at any rate there is perfect peace." White's linking different species of birds to different types of people is a suggestion from him that the reader do so himself with all of the other animals in the book (if he has not yet started doing so already). The explicit link between animals and humans is again reiterated near the end of Chapter 19, when the Wart flies over the town of birds, complete with crowded slums. Kay's clumsy entrance (bearing a dead thrush) reveals his complete ignorance of birds' more "human-like" qualities.

Archimedes proves himself to be another in the Wart's long list of teachers. Although his methods can be harsh (he reprimands the Wart for his flying method and calls him an "idiot"), he does achieve his desired results. As when the Wart was literally able to see the world differently as a perch in Chapter 5, the same phenomenon occurs here as an owl, when the Wart is able to see one ray beyond the visible spectrum. An even greater change of perception occurs when the Wart finds himself suddenly transformed into a wild goose. White's description of the air relies almost wholly on abstract language in order to convey the Wart's new and inexplicable sensation of flight. The Wart is described as feeling like "a point in geometry, existing mysteriously on the shortest distance between two points" and the sky is depicted as "a pulseless world-stream steady in limbo." These moments of new perception are literal examples of what is metaphorically occurring every time the Wart becomes a new animal and receives a new lesson.

While all of the animals into which the Wart is transformed throughout the novel are, to some degree, human, the geese are, without question, the most *humane*. Their beauty and camaraderie is so great that the Wart is moved to sing; their *joie de vivre*" is such that the Wart cannot but help become entranced by his new surroundings. Lyo-lyok, as another teacher, is patient and good-humored, helping the Wart with his duties as sentry; however, her amusement over the Wart's human nature turns to horror when he asks her about the sentries and if they are currently "at war." Her initial inability to understand the Wart's question—followed by her distaste at what he means by "at war"—suggests a compassion and basic decency in the geese that humans are supposed to possess but too often do not. Her question, "But what creature could be so low as to go about in bands, to murder others of its own blood?" is supposed to be hypothetical, but does, of course, have a ready answer: man. The geese are the complete opposite of the warlike ants that the Wart encountered in Chapter 8: They have no use for war because, in the air, there are no boundaries and, therefore, no causes for battle. They have no Kings, no laws, and their only private properties are their nests. Despite what the reader understands at this point, however, the Wart is still ignorant of Lyo-lyok's teaching, calling fighting "knightly." Her explanation of his attitude ("you're a baby") suggests the degree to which the Wart still must change before he becomes King.

Theme

Before ending the episode, White inserts an anecdote concerning the inherent dignity and natural leadership abilities of geese. This story (which White says "ought to make people think") suggests the link between the Wart's future as King and his present situation as a wild goose: Knowing what he does about animals (everything), Merlyn would, undoubtedly, want his pupil to learn of real leadership and how it works. While the Wart does not hear the anecdote about the farmer and his henhouse directly, the principle behind it—that leaders take charge when a leader is needed—is embodied in the geese that the Wart meets on his migration across the North Sea. The ants' leaders exist merely to begin wars, but the admirals of the geese lead their flocks above and beyond the boundaries that cause so much conflict.

Glossary

Chapter 17

Gilbert White a minister and observer of nature (1720–1793).

Quaker a member of the Society of Friends, a Christian movement noted for plain dress and simple living.

chaffinch a small European finch that has a white patch on each shoulder.

Linnaeus Carolus Linnaeus (1707–1778), Swedish botanist.

kestrel a small, reddish-gray European falcon.

shrikes predatory, shrill-voiced passerine birds with hooked beaks, gray, black, and white plumage, and long tails.

Proserpine the mythical daughter of Zeus, abducted by Pluto to be the Queen of Hades, but allowed to return to the earth for part of the year. She is sometimes used as a personification of Spring.

Chapter 18

Alderbaran, Betelgeuse, and Sirius three stars.

Orion a constellation named after a mythical hunter.

atomy a tiny being.

the lower strata the lower layer of the atmosphere.

purgatory a place of limbo, traditionally believed to be located between Heaven and Hell.

joie de vivre French for "joy of living."

maritime of or relating to sea navigation.

heather a type of heath-grass with small purple flowers.

widgeon a freshwater duck.

curlew a large, brownish shorebird.

redshanks and dunlin types of European sandpipers.

tussocks thick tufts or clumps of grass.

anseriformes geese.

peregrines falcons used for hawking.

blue-stocking a learned, bookish, or pedantic woman.

Chapter 19

guillemot a shorebird.

kittiwake a small gull.

W. H. Hudson English naturalist and writer (1841–1922).

Chapters 20–21

Summary

Six years pass. Although the Wart's education has continued and he has been transformed into countless different animals, he has grown melancholy and jealous of Kay's impending knighthood. Kay, of course, has no concern for the Wart's feelings and remains a stubborn and sarcastic young man. Merlyn consoles the Wart by telling him that "only fools want to be great," but the Wart pays him no heed, instead telling Merlyn how he would behave, given the chance to be knighted.

The week before Kay's knighting ceremony, Merlyn delivers him one last lecture on the value of education and begins the Wart's last lesson by transforming him into a badger. On his way to the badger hole, the Wart meets a frightened hedgehog, who describes the terrors that the badgers inflict upon him and his kind, as well as the kindness shown to him by Merlyn. When the Wart meets the badger, he is asked to listen to the badger's treatise on why Man has become master of the animals. After he hears the badger's argument, the Wart reveals that he has not, in fact, wholly understood the point.

Commentary

Although the Wart has grown into a teenager and has had the benefit of Merlyn's tutoring for six years, he is still, in many ways, a boy. His jealousy of Kay's future honors is understandable, but his blind devotion to Kay (who mocks the Wart's parentage and rank as a squire) suggests a mind less sophisticated than one may expect. Even White himself describes the Wart as "stupid," which, in this context, also means "naïve" and "boyish." Clearly, the Wart's education is not yet complete, which is why White has him approach Merlyn to receive his final lesson. Merlyn attempts to dispel the Wart's worship of Kay by describing the knighting ritual in a sardonic and dismissive tone: He calls it "only a lot of fuss" and says that Kay will hear "a long lecture about the ideas of chivalry such as they are." The Wart, however, recognizes none of Merlyn's sarcasm and speaks so prophetically to his teacher that the irony is unmistakable: "If I were to be made a knight . . . I should pray to God to let me encounter all the evil in the world in my own person, so that if I conquered there would be none left, and, if I were defeated, I would be the one to suffer for it."

The Wart's idealism here is, indeed, admirable, but unlike the reader and Merlyn, he cannot recognize his folly in asking for such a fate. As King Arthur, the Wart *will* encounter "all the evil in the world" and *will* "be the one to suffer" when he is defeated; Merlyn knows this and also knows of the pain which will eventually come to his pupil. However, the reader does see a tender side of Merlyn in this scene that is not found elsewhere in the novel: Because he cannot reveal the Wart's fate to him, Merlyn must ultimately say nothing and sit silently, with his beard in his mouth, staring "tragically" into the fire. His concern over the eventual destruction of his pupil's lofty ideals disturbs the usually pragmatic wizard.

Merlyn does, however, rouse himself from his concerns to give the Wart his final lesson. .In the wizard's final lecture, the reader can detect the voice of White himself, articulating his most important theme: The glory of knighthood may burn bright, but the fires of education burn longer. This idea (of the inherent good in learning) is—more than any of the Wart's individual transformations into animals—Merlyn's greatest lesson and the one he most wants the Wart to digest

Theme

Of all the animals into which the Wart comes in contact, the badger is the most obviously depicted as an embodiment of learning: He takes the Wart to a room resembling an Oxford or Cambridge study hall, complete with gowns, portraits of departed alumni badgers "famous in their day for scholarship," and "a portrait of the Founder over the fireplace." This is the first literal classroom into which the Wart has stumbled and it is here that he will receive his most offbeat lesson, because it is one about Man himself.

Again the Wart hears a parable: According to the badger, God summoned all of the embryos of all the animals before Him and offered them all the opportunity, before He "finished" them, to alter any of their features. All of the animals asked for changes in their hands, teeth, or hides in order to better survive in the wild. Man, however, preferred not to offend God and be "rude" by implying (through the request for an alteration) that there was some kind of flaw in His design. Delighted, God proclaimed that man "is the only one who has guessed Our riddle," and conferred upon him "the Order of Dominion" over all of the earth's creatures.

The issues raised in the parable resonate throughout *The Sword in the Stone*, and it is important to first identify these issues as White suggests them here. Because Man remains in an "embryonic" state, he is, in a figurative sense, childlike—untouched yet naive. More importantly, Man will remain "eternally undeveloped" and exist as "potential." In other words, Man will never be "finished" in any biological (or moral) sense of the word. He will always need to strive to improve himself, which causes God to feel "partly sorry" for him—yet this constant striving for perfection also causes God to feel "partly hopeful." The parable explores the duality of Man: an animal of near-divine potential and capacity for greatness, yet also one who squanders his "Order of Dominion" by engaging in acts of violence that threaten the very world he rules.

All through *The Sword in the Stone*, the reader finds examples of the parable's ideas. The entire institution of chivalry is a conscious attempt on the part of men to better themselves through the enacting of noble deeds; but men being what they are, the aims of chivalry are often thwarted by greed, ambition, and idleness. Thus, Man strives for perfection but is often undercut by his own failings—even a scene as silly as the joust between Grummore and Pellinore in Chapter 7 illustrates this point. Similarly, Kay's impending knighthood should make him a better person; instead, he becomes more stubborn and nasty than ever before.

At this point in his development, the Wart is all potential and exists as a figurative "embryo" in the world of chivalry, politics, and leadership. The final conversation between the Wart and the badger suggests just how embryonic the Wart remains, even at this late date in his education. When the badger points out the fact that Man possesses "a quantity of vices," the worst of which is his tendency to engage in warfare, the Wart fervently (and without any thought) defends his own species. Even when the badger points out that only five (of the four thousand) species of ant, one termite, and Man kill their own kind, the Wart states that he "would have liked to go to war" so that he could revel in "the banners, the trumpets, the flashing armour and the glorious charges." Like Lyo-lyok before him, the badger earnestly tries to impress upon the Wart the horror of war, but the boy is still (as Lyo-lyok called him) "a baby" or, in this context, an embryo. The badger's last question to the Wart—"Which did you like best, the ants or the wild geese?"—seems like a change of subject, but can also be read as an interrogation of the Wart's values: "Would you" (the question asks) "rather live in a world revolving around war or one in which war does not exist?" White does not have the Wart answer the question because, at this stage, he cannot answer it: He lacks the sophistication necessary to infer the badger's point. He is, like Adam in the parable, still a creature of "potential."

Glossary

Chapter 20

sciatica any painful condition in the region of the hip and thigh.

ewers pitchers with wide mouths.

frumenty a English dish of hulled wheat boiled in milk, sweetened, and flavored with spice.

Chapter 21

canary a fortified wine similar to Madeira, made in the Canary Islands.

milliard a billion.

the Little Bear a constellation, also known as the Little Dipper.

tumulus an artificial mound.

crofter one who rents and works on a small farm.

midden a dunghill or refuse heap.

the drouthy antipodes a group of cold, drafty ("drouthy") islands belonging to New Zealand.

Chapters 22–24

Summary

The day before Kay is to be knighted, Pellinore arrives at Sir Ector's and informs him that the King, Uther Pendragon, has died without an heir. He also explains that, in London, a sword has mysteriously appeared that passes through an *anvil* (a heavy blacksmith's block on which he bangs pieces of metal) and then into a stone. The inscription on the pommel reads, "Whoso Pulleth Out This Sword of this Stone and Anvil, is Rightwise King Born of All England." On New Year's Day, Pellinore explains that a tournament will be held so that all the men of England can try to remove the sword. Kay asks his father if they may visit the capital for the tournament, and Sir Ector eventually agrees. The Wart, unaware of the events in London and brokenhearted at Merlyn's announcement that he is leaving, then enters with his tutor.

Sir Ector and his boys travel to London for the tournament. When Kay arrives at the tilting grounds, he realizes he has forgotten his sword and sends the Wart (now his squire) back to their inn to retrieve it. Finding the inn locked and no one inside, the Wart desperately searches for a replacement sword. He approaches the sword in the stone (having no idea of its significance) and, after a struggle, removes it. (All of his animal friends watch and coach him as he makes his attempts.) When he brings it to Kay and tells of how he got it, Kay lies to his father and says that he (Kay) pulled it out of the stone. Kay eventually confesses that the Wart pulled it out. Ector and Kay then fall to their knees and hail the Wart as their new King. The Wart, confused and embarrassed, bursts into tears.

The novel ends with the Wart's coronation and a party that is thrown after it. All of the characters attend the party and bring the Wart a number of gifts. The last gift is given by Ector: a cone that looks like a dunce cap that is lit at one end, which turns into Merlyn. The magician explains that Uther Pendragon was the Wart's father; Merlyn knew this, of course, but was forbidden to mention it to the boy. Merlyn then asks the privilege of being the first of the Wart's subjects to address him with his new tittle: King Arthur. Merlyn also reassures his new King that he will stay with him for a long time.

Commentary

Kay's desire to attend the tournament in London reflects his desire for fame and the cultivation of his reputation. According to him, "anybody who does not go for a tournament like this will be proving that he has no noble blood in his veins." He feels that he must "have a shot" at the sword, or people will say "Sir Ector's family was too vulgar and knew it had no chance." When he arrives in London, he is even more egotistical, offering the Wart a shilling to fetch his sword, as if he is the Lord of a manor tipping a carriage-driver or servant. The greatest display of his need for fame occurs when he lies to his father by claiming that he (and not the Wart) removed the sword from the stone.

In these final chapters, as in the rest of the novel, the Wart is a direct contrast to his brother. While Kay worries about impressing the public in London, the Wart cries over the announcement of Merlyn's departure. Kay frets over appearing noble at the tournament, while the Wart pulls the sword from the stone without any understanding of his impending greatness. Also note that Kay is quick to lie and claim the honors of having removed the sword, while the Wart begins to cry when he realizes he will be King. This is, perhaps, an unexpected response, but one must remember that the Wart does not covet power or the chance to lord his new position over anybody. However, Kay does redeem himself by admitting that the Wart pulled out the sword—to a degree, he, too, has evolved along with his brother.

Literary Device

The scene in which the Wart removes the sword is like his "graduation" from the program of studies he has followed since boyhood. All the animals he has befriended arrive to cheer him on as he pulls at the sword. White stresses the fact that all the animals in attendance "had come to help on account of love"; the Wart is not especially strong or savvy—but he does endear others to him, and the combined power of all of their love allows the Wart to feel "his power grow." These citizens of his kingdom love him already, and their human counterparts will feel the same way.

The detailed list of gifts given to the Wart reads like a summary of the Wart's life since the beginning of the novel. Some of the gifts are reminiscent of his adventures (Robin and Marian give him a gown made from pine martens); some are touching (Cavil gives him "his heart and soul," Kay gives his own record griffin, "with honest love"); and some are outright jokes on White's part (Pellinore and the Questing Beast send some of their "most perfect fewmets"). The Lord Mayor and Alder-men's gift of a spacious "aquarium-mews-cum-menagerie" underscores the importance that the animals have played in the Wart's education.

Merlyn's having the last words in the novel is certainly just, because he engineered the Wart's entire education. His gift—a promise to stay with the Wart—is the most valuable of them all, and his final confir-mation that he will stay reflects the novel as a whole: "Yes, Wart. Or rather, as I should say (or is it have said?), Yes, King Arthur." In a book filled with transformations, this is the greatest one: A simple boy whose nickname suggests his unimportance is transformed into the man hold-ing the most powerful title in England. After becoming a perch, hawk, ant, goose, and badger, the Wart has become King Arthur.

Glossary

Chapter 22

standards, banners, pennons, pennoncells, banderolls, guidons, streamers and cognizances different decorative flags and ribbons used to adorn the castle.

lollards any of the followers of John Wycliffe in fourteenth- and fif-teenth-century England.

pommel the knob on the end of the hilt of some swords and daggers.

Some red propaganda "Some communist propaganda."

Chapter 23

palfrey a saddle horse.

hostelry inn.

Punch and Judy English puppets known for slapstick humor.

hurdy-gurdy an early instrument shaped like a lute or violin but played by turning a crank attached to a rosined wheel that causes the strings to vibrate.

wote know.

wend thought.

seneschal a steward or major-domo in the household of a medieval noble.

Chapter 24

burghers inhabitants of a borough or town.

given an angel each an "angel" is a medieval coin bearing a figure of the archangel Michael piercing a dragon.

char-a-banc a coach.

Aldermen members of an English borough council.

beys a Turkish title of respect and former title of rank.

mahatmas in India, those of a class of wise and holy persons held in special regard or reverence.

The Queen of Air and Darkness

Like the other volumes in *The Once and Future King*, *The Queen of Air and Darkness* begins with an epigraph: "When shall I be dead and rid / Of the wrong my father did? / How long, how long, till spade and hearse / Put to sleep my mother's curse?"

The pleading questions asked here are never directly posed by the Wart (now King Arthur) in the novel; however, the sense of the "sins of the fathers" affecting the son—and the past affecting the present—is a chief component of the Arthurian legend (and White's retelling of it). Throughout *The Queen of Air and Darkness*, Arthur struggles to reform and "civilize" the bloody nation (torn by racial strife) left to him by his father, Uther Pendragon. However, as White implies before the book even begins, the time when Arthur will be "dead and rid" of the troubles engendered by his father's (and other Normans') tyranny may be slow in coming—or never arrive at all. The focus of the novel is war, but the war fought here is one that has origins in the distant past. To "put to sleep" the problems plaguing his country, Arthur revolutionizes his own (and other characters') thinking about wars, their origins, and who fights in them. Seen in this light, *The Queen of Air and Darkness* is, like *The Sword in the Stone*, a tale of Arthur's education. As he learned of the horrors of war in the first volume, he puts his learning into practice in the second, attempting to actually eradicate war completely from his nation.

Arthur's revolutionary theory of entering and then winning a "war to end all wars" does not occur to him instantly, early in his reign. When the novel begins, Arthur is still very much like the Wart he was in *The Sword in the Stone*. White introduces him with the description, "He had fair hair and a stupid face, or at any rate there was a lack of cunning in it." Even Merlyn has become restless and impatient with his pupil: When Arthur asks Merlyn if he has "been doing something wrong," the wizard replies, "It is not so much what you are doing . . . It is how you are thinking. If there's one thing I can't stand, it's stupidity." The "stupidity" that so infuriates Merlyn is not of an academic strain; rather, he detests Arthur's ideas about war and violence, which are revealed to him when the King describes his battle with Lot of Orkney as "splendid." After his boyhood lessons, Arthur should know better than to use such a word to describe a thing so terrible; however, Arthur is still like a schoolboy in many ways, including his conception of war. Merlyn must again become his tutor so that the King can think for himself after the wizard is locked "in a hole" (as he will be by Nimue) later in life.

To make his student rethink his ideas about the "splendid" nature of war, Merlyn offers Arthur a brief history lesson in which he outlines the last three thousand years of military conflict. When Arthur calls Sir Bruce Sans Pitie a "swine" and a "marauder," he fails to realize that a man like Sir Bruce is simply "an example of the general situation." A long time ago, the Gaels who fought with copper hatchets were defeated by another clan of Gaels with bronze swords, who were then driven West by Teutons with iron weapons, who were themselves attacked by the Romans and, eventually, the Saxons. The Saxons, however, were then conquered by the Normans, leaving the present situation in which the Gaels resent the Gauls (their Norman oppressors) and see Arthur's coronation as a "chance to pay off racial scores, and to have some blood-letting as sport, and to make a bit of money in ransoms." The universal thinking that "Might is Right" disgusts the wizard, who contends that wars are "the greatest wickedness of a wicked species." "There is no excuse for war," he explains, "and whatever the wrong which your nation might be doing to mine—short of war—my nation would be in the wrong if it *started* a war so as to redress it." Merlyn's words here recall those of Lyo-lyok, the wild goose, who tells Arthur in *The Sword in the Stone* that he is a "baby" because he finds war a "knightly" pursuit.

Theme

What infuriates Merlyn even more than the savagery of war, however, is the complete and nonchalant acceptance of it as an institution wherein nobles, fully protected in armor, exploit the lower classes out of greed and even boredom. He cites various battles where the nobles applied the rules of sport and etiquette to the death of their own people, such as that of King Henry II, who borrowed money from his opponent in order to continue fighting him. This thinking of war as something to be "indulged" in "seasonally" is presented by Merlyn as morally repugnant. Using his knowledge of the future, he compares war to a Victorian foxhunt—an activity that's fun and exhilarating for the hunters (the nobles) but terrifying and violent for the foxes (the soldiers who actually die in battle). A foxhunt's only purpose is to entertain leisured aristocrats (a fox is not eaten nor killed for any real reason), so warfare's only purpose is to inflate the egos of a masculine and violent band of nobles. He tells Arthur: "You have become the king of a domain in which . . . the nobility fight each other for fun, and neither the racial maniac nor the overlord stops to consider the lot of the common soldier, who is the one person that gets hurt. Unless you can make the world wag better than it does at present, King, your reign will be an endless series of petty battles . . . ."

As other parts of the novel demonstrate (such as Igrane's sons torturing the donkey and later butchering the unicorn), human beings have a seemingly innate capacity for violence. Merlyn wants Arthur to understand that there is nothing "splendid" in war or those who boast of their prowess in entering it.

Character Insight

Thus, Arthur's triumph in *The Queen of Air and Darkness* is more mental than military. After seriously considering Merlyn's argument, the King is finally able to think for himself and come to the conclusion that "the last battle we had—in which seven hundred kerns were killed—was not so much fun as I thought it was" and that "battles are not fun when you come to think about them." This epiphany may strike some readers as obvious, but these readers should recall that Arthur is not living in a twentieth-century democracy; he is a product of the feudal system and a world that, in every economic, political, and social way, continually asserts the idea that "Might is Right." *Kerns*, what the military today might call "common soldiers," are seen by Arthur's contemporaries as expendable; Arthur, of course, thinks differently. His thinking here is a breakthrough, akin to Galileo's idea that the Earth revolves around the Sun—and just as shocking and dangerous to his opponents. Arthur conjectures that people are "half horrible and half nice," but they often let themselves "run wild," in part due to their "Norman idea about the upper classes having a monopoly of power, without reference to justice."

Arthur plans to "harness Might so that it works for Right"—in other words, he will fight the upcoming battle of Bedegraine in order to stop people from thinking of war as he once did. As World War I was called "The War To End All Wars" and viewed, in its time, as an event that would destroy the old world to make way for new progress in humanity, so Arthur plans to win this last battle in order to institute his own idea of order: chivalry, whose oath will be "Might is only to be used for Right." The King has freed himself from the clichéd notions of war held so dear by other nobles, and has formulated a new world order. This conclusion is exactly the one that Merlyn wanted Arthur to draw, for after he hears the King explain it, he begins reciting the Nunc Dimitis: a canticle beginning with the words, "Lord, now lettest thou thy servant depart in peace." The wizard is at peace because the King will bring peace to the nation and attempt to right the wrongs mentioned in the epigraph.

White's description of the battle of Bedegraine stresses the ways in which Arthur's new concept of war is put into practice. According to the nobles' custom, a "good war had to be full of 'arms shoulders and heads flying about the field and blows ringing by the water and the wood.' But the arms, shoulders, and heads would be those of villeins, and the blows which rang, without removing many limbs, would be exchanged by the iron nobility." Such is the idea of warfare held by Arthur's opponents, the Eleven Kings. He orders that there will be no ransoms and that his knights will only fight other knights, observing no "ballet-dancer's rules." They are to "press the war home to its real lords—until they themselves" are "ready to refrain from warfare, being confronted with its reality." Arthur is waging war on an idea as much as on another army. White's tone in describing the battle suggests his endorsement of Arthur's thinking. He frequently becomes sarcastic (Arthur begins with an "atrocity" by "not waiting for the fashionable hour") and adopts the point-of-view of Arthur's enemies to display their foolishness in still thinking of war like a foxhunt. When Arthur chases his enemies' nobles without their own footmen, "They were indignantly surprised by what they considered an unchivalrous personal outrage—outrageous to be attacked with positive manslaughter, as if a baron could be killed like a Saxon kern." White even states that Arthur's "second atrocity was that he neglected the kerns themselves," instead "concentrating his indignation upon the leaders who had seduced their addled pates." King Lot realizes too late that he is being faced with "a new kind of warfare" which holds that "the death of gentlemen" is an acceptable part of battle. Because he ignores the traditional ways of thinking about war, Arthur gains an easy victory over the Eleven Kings. To recall the issue raised in the epigraph, the future of warfare (embodied by Arthur) defeats the past (embodied by the Eleven Kings), creating a peaceful present in which nobles who begin wars are taken to task for risking the lives of their own subjects. The foxhunt is over, at least for the moment.

While Arthur's growth in the novel is exemplary, however, he is still not free from other forms of malice. Although he has revolutionized warfare, refuted the accepted wisdom that "Might is Right," and conceived of the Knights of the Round Table, he is still a man and therefore still prey to human weaknesses. As soon as his guard is relaxed and he sits in his Great Hall, contemplating the peace he is sure will come to England, he is seduced by Queen Morgause, the novel's title character. Their unholy union will engender Mordred, who, in turn, will topple Camelot from all its glory and reinstitute the "Might is Right"

way of thinking. So as the epigraph concerns the sins of the fathers, White tells the reader (in the novel's last paragraph) that Mordred's birth is what makes the Arthur legend a tragedy of "sin coming home to roost." Although dubbed "The War To End All Wars," World War I was followed by an even more bloody and terrible conflict twenty-one years later; similarly, after creating a "new kind of warfare" to prevent future conflict, Arthur still brings about his own, inevitable destruction. As White concludes, "He did not know he was doing so, and perhaps it may have been due to her, but it seems, in tragedy, that innocence is not enough." The novel is therefore named after Queen Morgause because it is she who, in her own secret way, eventually plants the seeds that will destroy Arthur's reign, just as World War I, in its own way, paved the way for an even more horrifying sequel.

The Ill-Made Knight

As *The Sword in the Stone* examines educational issues and *The Queen of Air and Darkness* explores political ones, *The Ill-Made Knight* is a novel whose focus is love—including, but not limited to, the forbidden love of Lancelot and Guenever. The novel abounds in different strains of love and lovers. There is, foremost, Lancelot and Guenever's affair, but there is also Arthur's blind love of his best knight, Gawaine; Agravane's violent love of their mother; Merlyn's inescapable love for Nimue; Elaine's hopeless (and eventually deadly) love for Lancelot; and Galahad's love of his own righteousness. However, the greatest love affair in this novel is not between Lancelot and Guenever, but between Lancelot and God, whose love eventually wins over the great knight. Thus, *The Ill-Made Knight* explores the ways that different kinds of love and devotion (to people, chivalry, and God) affect one's character, and how one man—Lancelot—struggles with the different loves in his heart until he finds peace in a love greater than any worldly affection.

Before examining the intricacies of Lancelot's heart, however, a reader may wonder why White devotes a whole volume of *The Once and Future King* to this particular character. Recall Arthur's idea (in *The Queen of Air and Darkness*) to reform his nation after quelling the present rebellions: "I will institute a sort of order of chivalry . . . And then I shall make the oath of the order that Might is only to be used for Right . . . The knights in my order will ride all over the world . . . but they will be bound to strike only on behalf of what is good . . . ."

Arthur's version of chivalry is one designed to make its practitioners more like God, who uses "Might" only on "behalf of what is good." (The quest for the Holy Grail emphasizes the spiritual nature of Arthur's denomination of chivalry.) Therefore, the more a knight fulfills the ideals of chivalry, the closer he grows to God. Lancelot is such a knight, invincible in combat and always ready to rescue any number of damsels in distress; however, he also succumbs to his own desires and places the wants of his own heart above those of God's. Like God, Lancelot wants a "Word," thinking it "the most valuable of possessions"; unlike God, however, he is unable to keep his "Word" and remains a fallible human.

Character Insight

This combination of the desire to attain divine godliness and the impurities of human nature marks Lancelot as the most interesting of Arthur's knights. Even more important is the idea that his contradictions also epitomize chivalry as a whole: a desire for men to reach impossible levels of goodness while, at the same time, struggling with their own fallibility. Thus, in Arthurian myth, Lancelot's sin is sleeping with the Queen—a sin that may not be the most heinous one imaginable but certainly a squalid and "unholy" one. Lancelot's giving in to his flesh reveals the "fallen" state of man as well as his need for something like chivalry to restore him to his former glory. As White explains, "It is the bad people who need principles to restrain them," and "bad," in this context, means "everybody," because even a man like Arthur's greatest knight can wander off the path of righteousness. Only Lancelot, the greatest, yet most "ill-made" knight, embodies the best and worst of chivalry and human nature, making his story a valuable part of the Arthurian myth.

Style & Language

Lancelot's relationship with chivalry—and his love for Arthur, its inventor—is complex. He trains for three years in order to join Arthur's order "because he was in love with it." Chivalry, he is sure, will give him the spiritual "push" he needs to remain in the good graces of God. Lancelot also hopes that chivalry will allow him to redeem some of his inadequacies: The opening chapter presents "the French boy" looking into the polished surface of a kettle-hat, "trying to find out who he was" and "afraid of what he would find." His unarticulated but identifiable fear here is being rebuffed by Arthur: "He was in love with him" and wants to prove himself worthy to the English king. His dream of a "beautiful well" reveals young Lancelot's self-doubts: "as soon as he stopped his lips toward it, the water sank away. It went right down to the barrel of the well, sinking and sinking from him so that he could not get it. It made him feel desolate, to be abandoned by the water of the well."

Literary Device

The beautiful water found in this well is the fulfillment of Arthur's chivalric ideals—throughout *The Ill-Made Knight*, Lancelot will come close to quenching is thirst for holiness, but (because of his own sins) will be forbidden to drink (an idea made apparent when Lancelot is allowed to see—but not approach—the Holy Grail). White repeatedly stresses Lancelot's physical unattractiveness (a new spin on the legend) in order to stress the knight's contradictory nature: He is the greatest in terms of heroics and tilting, but "ill-made" in terms of morality. His face reveals his soul. After he is knighted, the fact that Lancelot begins embarking on quests in order to avoid Guenever suggests that such adventures "were his struggles to save his honor, not establish it." As he becomes a knight to avoid the "ugliness" he fears lies within him, he uses chivalry to avoid committing a terrible (yet inevitable) sin. For his momentary victory over himself, God rewards him by letting him perform a miracle, as he always wanted, and Lancelot saves Elaine from the cauldron of boiling water. At this point, the greatest knight is very close to God and glories in his deep love of chivalry; White describes the miracle as "the turning point of his life."

However, the impact of this "turning point" fades over time, and, as everyone familiar with the legend knows, Lancelot betrays both Arthur and Arthur's ideals by sleeping with Guenever. Lancelot's moral compass becomes skewed; he sacrifices all for which he has worked and proven for the sake of worldly (rather than divine) love. However, Guenever's and Lancelot's love is never portrayed by White as unseemly or lustful (as is the seduction of Arthur by Morgause in *The Queen of Air and Darkness*). Instead, White implies that their love is as fated as that of Merlyn and Nimue: the tragedy of Camelot lies in this idea. Motivated by his having been tricked by Elaine into sleeping with her, Lancelot justifies his racing toward Guenever with the logic that "He was a lie now, in God's eyes as he saw them, so he felt that he might as well be a lie in earnest." He knows, as he approaches the Queen's bedchamber, that he will no longer be "the best knight in the world," have the power "to work miracles against magic," or have some "compensation for ugliness and emptiness in his soul." Her earthly love is too strong for him to resist and Lancelot finds the inevitability of his own fall quite painful: He tells the Queen, "I have given you my hopes, Jenny, as a present from my love." Fully aware of his betrayal of Arthur and of God, whose ideals are embodied by the King, Lancelot accepts the "ill-made" nature of his soul. "He believed as firmly as Arthur did, as firmly as the benighted Christian, that there is such a thing as Right." Because of this unshakable belief, Lancelot "loved Arthur" (who embodies Godliness) "and he loved Guenever" (who embodies human desire) "and he hated himself" (whom he views as a man unable to live up to the demands of his own ideals and conscience).

Theme

To this point, White's retelling of the affair keeps in fairly strict accordance with the legend. White's innovation, however, lies in his shifting the narrative at this point to how God enters Lancelot and Guenever's affair as a rival for the great knight's love. As *The Ill-Made Knight* proceeds, the presence of God becomes greater with each passing chapter, beginning with Lancelot's childhood desires to perform miracles, moving through Arthur's decision to (figuratively) "send you all to the Pope" on a crusade for the Grail, to the testing of Sir Bors and Sir Percivale, and finally to the discovery of the Grail by Galahad, whom Lancelot describes as an "angel."

God hovers in the background of the novel, just as His ideas, found in Arthur's chivalry, hover only in the background of Lancelot's soul as he commits the sin of adultery. After Lancelot returns from his two-year quest for the Grail, however, he describes the epiphany that refocused and clarified his relationship with God: a "stroke of a correction" for which he is thankful. Through a series of events, orchestrated by God, Lancelot realized that his worst sin was his very desire to be the greatest proponent of Arthur's chivalry. Even after confessing his affair with Guenever to a priest, Lancelot was still "beaten and disgraced" at a tournament, because, as he explains to the King and Queen: "It was pride that made me try to be the best knight in the world. Pride made me show off and help the weaker party of the tournament. You could call it vainglory. Just because I had confessed about—about the woman, that did not make me into a good man."

After confessing this sin, Lancelot was again knocked down, this time by a black knight. Guenever cannot understand why God would have allowed this to happen, if Lancelot "really was absolved this time." Lancelot's explanation—that God was not punishing him, but simply "withholding the special gift of victory which it had always been within His power to bestow"—is the core of his new relationship with God. It is a relationship that Guenever, a worldly woman, cannot understand, because it hinges on Lancelot having "given up" his glory to get nothing back. She lives in a world of *quid pro quo* (or "something for something") and lacks the insight that Lancelot, now touched by God, possesses. Because of his past sins, Lancelot is ultimately forbidden from entering the chapel where Galahad, Bors, and Percivale celebrate Mass with the Grail—but he does not resent God for this decision because he now recognizes his own sinful pride.

As mentioned earlier, God then becomes a rival of Guenever for Lancelot's love. Lancelot, in his "innocent love of God," attempts to hold on to his new, divine love, arguing to Guenever that "they could not very well go back to their old way, after the Grail" and that "had it not been for their guilty love, he might have been allowed to achieve the Grail." Guenever eventually recognizes Lancelot's newfound spirituality and tells him, "I feel as if I were sacrificing you, or us if you like, to a new sort of love." Lancelot still yearns for Guenever, however, and White presents this as the crux and key point of the entire Lancelot story.

Despite her initial understanding of Lancelot's epiphany, Guenever's need for human companionship eventually proves too strong for her. She finds the fact that "Lancelot persisted in remaining loyal to his Grail" simply unbelievable, and becomes a jealous and embittered castaway. Guenever can only think of love in terms of human qualities, and her bitterness dramatizes the issues at stake in the novel: worldly comfort at odds with spiritual grace. The fact that Lancelot *again* sleeps with Guenever (when he rescues her from Sir Meliagrance) only serves to stress the fickle, yet ironically earnest, nature of a man who knows what is right yet keeps turning away.

Even a novel with such a protagonist as Lancelot, whose allegiances are constantly shifting, has to end, and White meets the challenge of providing an ending in which Lancelot retains his ties to both the human and the divine forces that have governed his life. Sir Urre, a knight from Hungary, suffers from a curse in which none of his wounds can ever heal; he has come to Camelot because the only cure for his wounds is if "the best knight in the world had tended them and salved them with his hands." Everyone, including Arthur, is sure that Lancelot will be able to cure Sir Urre; however, Lancelot, who has fallen back into Guenever's bed, knows that he is far from "the best knight in the world" and is sure that his inability to cure the knight will be viewed, correctly, as his "punishment." When confronted with Sir Urre, Lancelot utters a short prayer in his mind: "I don't want glory, but please can you save our honesty?" The crowd erupts as Lancelot heals Sir Urre's wounds, but White offers his reader a different, final glimpse of Lancelot's triumph: "The miracle was that he was allowed to do a miracle."

Lancelot is overcome with tears because he has learned another fundamental truth about God: He still loves Lancelot, despite the knight's forsaking Him for the warmth of a worldly, human bed. The miracle here is a paradox (a human behaves in a divine way) because the love of God is paradoxical as well: A man (or Man) can fall—repeatedly—yet still receive the love (and even grace) of God. Lancelot's tears are those of joy, but not pride, because he has learned that even the "greatest knight in the world"—and all of his chivalric ideals—cannot ever reach the perfection of a God who offers the true, unconditional love for which humans are constantly in search.

As Sir Lionel remarks early in the novel, "Give me a man who insists on doing the right thing all the time, and I will show you a tangle which an angel couldn't get out of." What *The Ill-Made Knight* makes clear is that no man—not even the best—can do "the right thing all the time." Only God can make such a claim, and judging from what Lancelot tells Arthur and Guenever about pride, He would not ever make such a boast in the first place. Man's love, as seen in Guenever, is wonderful yet flawed; only God's love offers the moral perfection that chivalry attempts to replicate.

The Candle in the Wind

Near the end of this, the last volume of *The Once and Future King*, White offers his readers a short "obituary" of Arthur, the mythical figure whom he has examined through the course of four novels: "He was only a man who had meant well . . . But it had ended in failure."

Since his boyhood, Arthur has moved from being the Wart, a naive but earnest boy, to being King Arthur, a man whose destiny and ideals were to become forever associated with England, the Round Table, and the age of chivalry. White humanizes Arthur as "only a man who had meant well," but a reader of *The Candle in the Wind* knows that White is being modest for his protagonist's sake. For as *The Candle in the Wind* makes clear, Arthur was a man whose ideas about might, right, and law stood far ahead of those believed by all his opponents—and even some of his allies. True, Arthur's attempt to institute a "total justice" in his kingdom proves "too difficult" and he is defeated by Mordred's might, but his attempt ennobles him and his example, forever recorded by the young page, Tom Malory, will inspire generations. What is myth for if not to serve as a guide to behavior and a framework through which one can view very modern issues? As *The Iliad* invites its readers to think about the effects of war and *Paradise Lost* examines the cosmic battle between good and evil, *The Candle in the Wind* is ultimately the record of one man's rise against wanton and terrible force—and how, despite his own destruction at the hands of it, he triumphs morally, if not militarily.

All four volumes of White's series are concerned with the workings of Force Majeure: the idea that any dispute can (and will) be settled by means of physical force. When (in *The Sword in the Stone*) the Wart meets Mr. P., the despotic perch, he sees Force Majeure in action: Mr. P. will eat anyone he pleases, whenever he has the urge. When (in *The Queen of Air and Darkness*) Arthur institutes a new kind of warfare and is able to "harness Might so that it works for Right," he is sure that he is forging a new idea that will forever change the way men think of battle. In *The Ill-Made Knight*, Arthur's Round Table effectively destroys the notion of Force Majeure and convinces the strongest knights in the realm to use their strength only in the name of God. However, after godliness has been attained by the Round Table's representatives, "those who had achieved the Quest had become perfect and lost to the world, while those who had failed in it had soon returned no better." Arthur's final attempt at curbing Force Majeure—an all-inclusive Law that will "make a map of force, as it were, to bind it down"—is the subject of

The Candle in the Wind. Arthur thinks that the combination of "Customary, Canon, and Roman law" into "a single code which he hoped to call the Civil one," will finally end the bloodshed that Lyo-lyok, the goose who taught him about boundaries as a boy in *The Sword in the Stone*, found so horrifying.

Arthur's idea is a fine one and worthy of a king who so codified masculine aggression that it became an instrument for doing right. However, Arthur's civil law—like the sin of his sleeping with Morgause—eventually "comes home to roost" and forces its very inventor to apply it to the two people he loves most: Lancelot and Guenever.

Theme

Arthur knows that laws should not be invented simply to crush one's enemies, for in that way tyranny lies, and tyrants need no excuse for killing their enemies in the first place. Such thinking is why, when Lancelot advises Arthur to cut off Mordred's head "and be done with him," the king instantly refuses. The only way that Arthur can "keep clear of force is by justice," and the hard fact of justice is that, "Far from being willing to execute his enemies, a real king must be willing to execute his friends . . . And his wife." The function of law is to implement right without the presence of Force Majeure; for this to be done, those who wish to defer to law must be willing to have it applied without any consideration for their own individual passions. Thus, Lancelot and Guenever must become the test case of Arthur's civil law, else its entire premise is undermined. Any exceptions made for the king's friend and wife will make the law a joke and its inventor a tyrant, like Mordred, who has no use for justice and calls it something that Arthur "does to people" simply "to amuse himself."

Naturally, Arthur despairs of his predicament. As Lancelot in *The Ill-Made Knight* finds himself torn between two equally powerful forces (Guenever and God), Arthur here finds himself pulled by both his desire for justice and his love for his friend and wife. After being forced, by his own logic, to allow Mordred and Agravaine to catch Lancelot with Guenever, Arthur has no choice, as a monarch, but to try and convict them. As a husband and friend, however, he constantly betrays his partisan hopes, like a judge who will pass down a guilty verdict if he is forced but who also hopes that he will be prevented from doing so. To his credit, Arthur never gives in to his own heart: He knows that Gawaine will follow the banished Lancelot and eventually kill him, and Arthur sits by his window to view Guenever's execution, because if he does not do so, the punishment will not be "legal." Caught in the ironies of his own creation, Arthur loses hope of reconciling his heart with his law—until the king watches Lancelot rescue Guenever from the stake and betrays his delight in his banished friend's actions: "My Lancelot! I knew he would! . . . Look, he is coming up to the Queen. . . . We shall win, Gawaine—we shall win!"

Arthur, delighted over having his legal cake and eating it too, then calls for a drink and is certain that he has eluded the grasp of his law—until Mordred appears and sours the moment with the news that, during the course of the Queen's rescue, Lancelot killed Gareth and Gaheris, both unarmed. His son has caught Arthur in another legal bind, for if Arthur does not capture and then try Lancelot for these two murders, he again risks the belittling of his precious law. Of course, Mordred only evokes justice in an attempt to get Arthur out of the country and further his own political ends—but he knows that Arthur (a man infinitely more honorable than he) cannot renege on his law and will be forced to apply it to his friend a second time. Guenever shows a keen understanding of her husband's predicament when she explains to her lady-in-waiting, "The king likes Lancelot so much that he is forced to be unfair to him—for fear of being unfair to other people." If Arthur fails to bring Lancelot to justice for the deaths of Gareth and Gaheris, he is betraying these two subjects as well as the political foundation of his kingdom; the fact that Lancelot killed them accidentally is—like his friendship with Arthur—irrelevant. Justice is supposed to be blind.

Thus, Arthur is forced to follow Lancelot to France and allow Gawaine to seek revenge on his brothers' killer: Although the king has repeatedly asked for an end to blood feuds, he must acknowledge Gawaine's right to demand justice for his loss. Another legal snare is that Arthur must leave Mordred as Lord Protector while he is away; the fact that Mordred—ostensibly the most evil character in all four novels—cannot be stopped because he has not, technically, broken any law suggests the faith Arthur invests in it. After Mordred does overstep his legal boundaries, however, Arthur is free to pursue and battle with him: As with his previously discussed love for both Lancelot and the law, Arthur again is given license to act more according to his heart than his sense of legal prudence. Gawaine's final letter to Lancelot, in which he asks the ill-made knight for his forgiveness and to help Arthur defeat Mordred, reveals the impact of Arthur's law on one of his disciples. If a man as set on the use of Force Majeure as Gawaine can view the law as a better alternative, surely there is hope for a future end to violence.

But the present still plagues Arthur, who, in the novel's last scene, sits in his tent and ruminates over his life and achievements. These thoughts serve as both an effective summary of the volumes of *The Once and Future King* as well as White's last lecture to the reader on the terrors of a world governed only by Force Majeure—a world he had just witnessed during World War II. Although Arthur is described as a man whose idea was "doomed to failure," this description is a half-truth. True, the Law will not stop Mordred, who will slay his father after the novel ends. But as Arthur's thoughts continue, the reader detects White's linking these supposedly "medieval" ideas about war and law to the twentieth century, which is one of the overall aims of all myth and White's retelling of the Arthurian one. Arthur considers: "Perhaps man was neither good nor bad, was only a machine in an insensate universe . . . Perhaps there were no virtues . . . Perhaps Might was a law of Nature, needed to keep the survivors fit. Perhaps he himself . . . But he could challenge it no further."

Theme

A reader cannot but help detecting the voice of Darwin speaking through the king—a voice so disturbing to him that he does not even complete his last question, which is, that perhaps he himself was only a creation of Nature, designed to keep the survivors in order. Arthur's thinking, like the England of White's imagination, grows more modern as the novels progress. Mordred is a blueprint for Hitler (with his hatred of Gaels and Jews, swastika-like badges, and stormtrooper "Thrashers") who brings Camelot into the twentieth century with his guns—the times of knights dueling like nobles and not striking each other when they fall are no more. Force Majeure has returned and will obliterate Camelot and its leader. When Guenever figuratively remarks earlier in the novel, "Civilization seems to have become insane," she speaks as a prophet, foretelling the fall of the Round Table, but not the ideals that kept it intact.

Style & Language

What is crucial to remember, however, is that the destruction of Camelot and the rebirth of Force Majeure comes about as a direct result of Arthur's, Guenever's, and Lancelot's own actions. "Sin coming home to roost" is a phrase repeated throughout the volumes of *The Once and Future King*, and the fact that Arthur's own son destroys him symbolically suggests the capacity for self-destruction that lies within each of us—even the most noble and forthright humanitarians are cursed with the free will that can engender their own destruction. In his tent, Arthur thinks that perhaps Mordred and he are "nothing but figureheads to complex forces which seem to be under a kind of impulse." This impulse is the human movement toward civilization—but as Arthur notes in *The Ill-Made Knight*, "I suppose that all endeavors which are directed toward a purely worldly end, as my famous civilization was, contain within themselves the germs of their own corruption." Man contains within him the capacity for unparalleled goodness (witness the Quest for the Holy Grail) but an equal capacity for evil (as seen in Mordred's attempt to willingly commit the same acts as that of the mythical Oedipus).

And so Camelot, and Arthur's entire way of thinking, is likened by White to a candle in the wind, literally extinguished by the mechanized terrors of the very modern Mordred. However, Arthur's meeting with Tom Malory, who will eventually compose *Le Morte D'Arthur*, ensures that the candle will be relit and will burn, as an example for future knights who struggle for right in the face of blind force. One of Arthur's final ruminations concerns a day "where he would come back to Gramarye with a new Round Table." The history of the world has shown the rebirth of the Round Table several times (the Allied Forces in World War II being just one example) and proven that, while Arthur's flesh may have been taken to Avalon, his ideas have not. The series ends with the statement

EXPLICIT LIBER REGIS QUONDAM REGISQUE
FUTURI THE BEGINNING

to suggest that the death of Arthur may be the end of a book, but the beginning of a force of good in the world still at work today. Mordreds may come, but young Tom Malory's reporting of the Round Table will continue to inspire present-day knights to fight the Thrashers in whatever form they may arrive. Thus Arthur is both the "once" and "future" King.

CHARACTER ANALYSES FOR *THE SWORD IN THE STONE*

Wart

A first-time reader of White's novel may be surprised at his initial portrayal of King Arthur—arguably the most famous monarch in literature—as an unassuming, rustic boy. In fact, Arthur is known only by his diminutive nickname "the Wart" until the very end of the book, when Merlyn addresses him by his more famous title. He is, throughout the novel, like a medieval Huckleberry Finn, discovering his personality as it is revealed to him through a number of tests and triumphs.

White's reasons for calling the young Arthur "the Wart" reflect his overall portrayal of the young king. When the novel begins, the Wart is a naïve, impressionable, and seemingly inconsequential boy, living in the shadow of his older brother. While he could never imagine himself as a figure in a medieval romance, he certainly devours these legends wholeheartedly, as seen through his awe of King Pellinore when they meet in the forest. (He later tells Merlyn that his greatest wish is to wear a "splendid suit of armor" and call himself "the Black Knight.") The Wart's admiration for all those connected with knighthood and adventure (such as King Pellinore, Kay, Sir Grummore, and Robin Wood) marks him as a "born hero-worshipper," an ironic description for the person who is to become one of the most-often-worshipped legendary heroes. The Wart, however, never dreams that he—a foundling—can ever rise to such heights.

This sense of childlike wonder makes the Wart an apt pupil for Merlyn's lessons. Throughout all of his tutorials with Merlyn, the Wart remains wide-eyed and receptive. Unlike Kay, who is often stubborn and selfish, the Wart is genuinely interested in the people (or, in his case, the animals) that he meets. This desire to learn about the beliefs and values of others will mark him as a fair and upright king—which the other volumes of White's saga confirm.

The fact that the Wart "becomes" King Arthur while fetching a sword for Kay is significant: Until the very moment where his destiny is revealed to him, the Wart remains subservient, eager to please others. When he pulls the sword from the stone and sees Ector and Kay kneel before him, the Wart begins to cry—unlike his brother, the Wart cannot imagine himself the recipient of great fame or renown. While he did confess to Merlyn that he would have liked to have been a knight, that was (in the Wart's mind) just a fantasy. White, however, views the Wart's sincerity and lack of presumption as his two greatest assets, contributing to the "reward" he receives at the end of the novel.

Merlyn

In a novel where the education of the protagonist propels its plot and development of its characters, the teacher-figure is of great importance. Merlyn, the Wart's teacher, is crucial to the young hero's growing maturity and political awareness. Like many good teachers, he challenges his pupil's values and assumptions about a number of important issues, such as friendship, government, and war. Throughout *The Sword in the Stone*, Merlyn imparts to the Wart the wisdom a king needs if he is to rule successfully.

When the Wart and the reader meet Merlyn, however, he seems more absent-minded than wise. He is first seen struggling with a bucket and dappled in bird droppings; his cottage is strewn with books and other trappings of wizardry. This seemingly chaotic setting, however, makes Merlyn less foreboding (and thus less threatening) to the Wart, and if a student is to learn anything, his teacher must not intimidate him.

Merlyn's methods are striking because he never *presents* nor *describes* a political system or point-of-view to the Wart—instead, he has the Wart *experience* life in the various systems as one of the many animals into which he transforms him. Turning the Wart into a perch, for example, allows him to meet Mr. P. and see firsthand the nature of tyranny; having the Wart spend a night in the mews teaches him about courage and military honor. Each of Merlyn's lessons has a similar goal, and Merlyn's ultimate aim is to ready the Wart for his impending role as King Arthur. By the end of *The Candle in the Wind*, however, Merlyn has almost wholly vanished from Arthur's life—but not from his memory, for the wizard's lessons remain with the king throughout his tumultuous reign.

Kay

Although Kay is the Wart's brother, he is his opposite (or *foil*) in many ways. One of the first descriptions of Kay informs the reader that he is "too dignified to have a nickname," and it is Kay's yearning for chivalric dignity that serves as the foundation of his character. He disregards the advice of those he deems lower than himself (such as Hob), despite the fact that he sometimes makes himself appear foolish in the process (as he does when disregarding Cully's advice about hawking). Kay is determined to become a knight, but lacks one of a knight's most important characteristics: humility. After killing a griffin, for example,

Kay revels in his father's mounting the head and placing a sign under it reading, "KAY'S FIRST GRIFFIN." Kay also has a tantrum when the Wart refuses to tell him about one of his lessons with Merlyn, and releases his envy in the punches he throws at his younger brother.

White emphasizes Kay's childishness at the novel's end, where Kay arrives in London to attempt to pull the sword from the stone. Naturally, Kay thinks he has a very good chance of doing so—an idea stressed when he thinks, "anybody who does not go for a tournament like this will be proving that he has no noble blood in his veins." He barks orders at the Wart to fetch his sword (as if the Wart were his slave rather than his squire) and even attempts to take credit for the Wart's pulling the sword from the stone. However, even a person as envious as Kay cannot deny the truth of the Wart's destiny, and must acknowledge him as King Arthur along with the rest of England.

Sir Ector

The father of the Wart and Kay, Sir Ector is a gruff but lovable father who (like many fathers) wants to raise his boys according to strict rules of conduct and the highest ideas that an "eddication" can offer. However, Sir Ector's idea of education consists of learning "Latin and stuff," which is a fine pursuit but not the most pressing one for a future king.

White often uses Sir Ector as a symbol of "merrie Englande," an era long past where knights and squires drank port, sang songs of heroic deeds, and attended tournaments. The novel opens with Sir Ector and Sir Grummore sharing a bottle of port and discussing the boys' need of a tutor. The episode in Chapter 15, in which Sir Ector and his friends listen to a songs on Christmas night, further portrays him as a kind-hearted remnant of a bygone age—an age that, by the end of *The Candle in the Wind* (the fourth volume of *The Once and Future King*), has given way to the forces of war and destruction.

CRITICAL ESSAY

A Guide to Arthurian Films

Because of their larger-than-life characters, the Arthurian legends have been widely adapted into films. What follows is a guide to some filmed versions of the Arthurian legend; each entry analyzes the issues raised by the film's director and how he adapts the Arthurian legend to suit his own artistic ends.

Excalibur (1981)

Directed by John Boorman; Screenplay by John Boorman and Rospo Pallenberg; Featuring Gabriel Byrne (Uther Pendragon), Nicol Williamson (Merlyn), Nigel Terry (King Arthur), Cherie Lunghi (Guenever), Nicholas Clay (Lancelot), Helen Mirren (Morgana), Robert Addie (Mordred), Liam Neeson (Gawaine), Paul Geoffrey (Perceval), and Patrick Stewart (Leondegrance).

Before the action of *Excalibur* begins, the viewer sees a title reading, "The Dark Ages. The land was divided, without a king. Out of these lost centuries rose a legend . . . Of the sorcerer, Merlin . . . Of the coming of a king . . . And of the sword of power . . . Excalibur." The sword of power being given prominence here (as well as the title of the film) reflects Boorman's overall vision of the legend: His film is a dark, somber, and often violent one, where passions run unrestrained and where power is sought and bargained for at great costs. Unlike White, who often opts for gentle irony and domestic touches, Boorman tells the story as a full epic, replete with dazzling costumes, operatic music, and battle scenes reminiscent of the Biblical films of the 1950s. If his version of the Arthurian legend sometimes lacks the sense that its characters are humans with feet of clay, it compensates for this by making them archetypes of lust (Uther), beauty (Guenever), evil (Morgana), temptation (Lancelot), saintliness (Perceval), wisdom (Merlin), avarice (Mordred), and nobility (Arthur). Boorman's arranging of scenes in which these characters interact and clash continually reinforces his theme of the human lust for power.

While *The Sword in the Stone* begins with Arthur as a boy, *Excalibur* first tells the story of Uther Pendragon, Arthur's father who conceives him during a night of deceptive love with Igraine, Cornwall's wife. (This is where Malory's *Le Morte D'Arthur* begins.) Boorman stresses the strength of Uther's lust: After making peace with Cornwall and uniting the land under his kingship, he is ready to forsake all he has won for a single night with his new ally's wife. He calls upon Merlin to transform him into the likeness of her husband so that she will not know she is being tricked—a proposition to which Merlyn agrees, provided that "the issue" of Uther's lust shall be his. After Arthur is born, however, Uther attempts to renege on his promise and love his infant son, but Merlin rips the baby from Igraine's arms. As in White, Merlin knows the future and has made this particular bargain to restore peace to the land; he attempted to do this with Uther, but the king's passions made him rekindle the very fires that Excalibur (the sword given to him by Merlin) helped him extinguish. Only Merlin, who proves himself a humanitarian concerned with the restoration of order, can help undo the damage caused by Arthur's father.

Boorman's Arthur shares many of the qualities of White's protagonist. As a boy, he is naive and nervous; after he discovers his destiny as king he is embarrassed by Ector's and Kay's falling prostrate before him. When warned by Merlin of Guenever's future treachery, Arthur refuses to heed his tutor's words, provoking the magician to remark, "Love is deaf as well as blind." As a king forced to face the adultery of Lancelot and Guenever, he must (as he is in *The Candle in the Wind*) let his own law be tested on whom he calls, "The two people I love most." When Guenever asks him to champion her and he refuses on the grounds that he must act as judge, he explains, "My laws must bind everyone, high and low, or they are not laws at all." When she counters this with, "You are my husband," he replies, "I must be King, first." Like his novelistic counterpart, Arthur is pained yet trapped in the snares of his own law, and Lancelot's rescue of Guenever from shame relieves the king as it does in White's novel.

As Lancelot, Nicholas Clay strikes a handsome figure, unlike the less-than-perfect Lancelot of *The Ill-Made Knight*. Both Boorman and White, however, stress Lancelot's absence from the Round Table as a means for him to avoid his own desires; as White remarks in *The Ill-Made Knight*, Lancelot's quests "were his struggles to save his honor, not to establish it." Lancelot's longing for Guenever is repeatedly shown to the viewer through many shots of his pining away in the forest, looking out at the castle where his true love dwells; Guenever eventually meets Lancelot in the forest to consummate their affair. This pastoral paradise is toppled, however, by Arthur's discovery of them, naked and asleep in a grove. He raises Excalibur—but rather than sinking it into Lancelot's heart, he plunges the sword into the earth. When the lovers awake they know exactly Arthur's message: "The king without a sword,"

Lancelot exclaims. "The land without a king!" Boorman implies that Lancelot and Guenever's betrayal of Arthur has opened wide the door for evil to enter Camelot—and it is at this point in the film that Morgana seduces her brother by transforming herself into the likeness of Guenever. Her using the same spell as Uther used to lie with her mother suggests the truth of what Merlin remarks early in the film: "It is the doom of men that they forget." Deception, like history, repeats itself.

Mordred is as sarcastic and spoiled in *Excalibur* as he is in *The Ill-Made Knight* and *The Candle in the Wind*. Born during a thunderstorm while his mother labors under the pain of her own evil, he is next shown as a giggling and malicious boy who leads Perceval to a tree where Arthur's other knights hang from nooses, with birds pecking at their faces. As a young man, he threatens his father, who is weakened from the collapse of his kingdom and the inability of his knights to find the Grail, with revolution. His father's plea, "I cannot give you the land— only my love" is met with, "That's the one thing of yours I don't want!" In White's novels, Mordred's evil is somewhat explained by the novelist's portrayal of Morgause, whose demanding yet distant nature makes her sons go to terrible extremes to win her approval; Boorman's Mordred is motivated by his quest for power. One of the only things the viewer hears him say to his mother is, "When will I be king?"

Ultimately, Boorman's film, like *The Candle in the Wind*, ends in triumph. As White's Arthur reviews his life the night before his death, Boorman's Arthur regains his strength (through the help of the Grail) and realizes that for much of his life, he has "been living through other people." He reconciles with Guenever (who has taken holy orders) and tells her, "I was not born to live a man's life, but to be the stuff of future memory." Guenever then restores Excalibur (which she has kept for many years) to Arthur's hand. Like White's Arthur, who hopes for a day "when he would come back to Graymarre with a new Round Table," Boorman's Arthur explains, "The fellowship was a brief beginning—a fair time that cannot be forgotten. And because it will not be forgotten, that fair time may come again." Although he meets his death soon after this pronouncement (in a graphic duel with Mordred), this cinematic Arthur remains more like a superhero than White's simple "man who meant well." His final voyage to Avalon, in the hands of the three queens, is inspiring, as the mist rises and the viewer (like Perceval, the only living witness) wonders when the glory of the Round Table will return to the "modern," Mordred-stricken world.

Camelot (1967)

Directed by Joshua Logan; Based on the stage play by Lana Jay Lerner and Frederick Lowe; Featuring Richard Harris (King Arthur), Vanessa Redgrave (Guenever), Franco Nero (Lancelot), David Hemmings (Mordred), and Lionel Jeffries (King Pellinore).

1960 marked the year of *Camelot*'s premiere on the Broadway stage; Lerner and Lowe's lavish musical proved to be as much of a success as their other works, *My Fair Lady* and *Brigadoon*. Starring Richard Burton as Arthur, Julie Andrews as Guenever, and Robert Goulet as Lancelot, the play ran for over 900 performances and earned two Tony awards. The play's title also came to be associated with the Kennedy White House and many people who had not even seen the play knew the refrain, "Cam-e-*lot*! Cam-e-*lot*!" In 1967, Joshua Logan directed the film version, an equally spectacular production starring Richard Harris as Arthur, Vanessa Redgrave as Guenever, and Franco Nero as Lancelot. Unlike *Excalibur*, with its violent battle scenes, dark tone, and largely pessimistic slant on the legend, *Camelot* often takes comic turns and ends long before Arthur's death. As *Excalibur* is named for the sword symbolizing the power that all of the characters struggle to possess, *Camelot* is named for the place that, although doomed to fall, remains an example of what men can accomplish when they strive for perfection.

Camelot is directly based on White's version of the Arthurian saga and a reader of *The Once and Future King* will recognize many of the elements of White's novels throughout the film. (Even minor characters such as King Pellinore and Uncle Dap make appearances.) However, Lerner and Lowe trimmed the scope of White's four novels in order to make the love triangle the center of the plot: The action of the film begins with Arthur meeting Guenever and ends the night before his attack on Joyous Gard (Lancelot's castle in France). Merlyn only appears in a few short flashbacks and Mordred, although still a major figure in the second half of the film, does not bring his armies and thrashers to England. The emphasis on Lancelot and Guenever's betrayal heightens the main issue raised in the film (and in the latter volumes of White's series): the struggle of a man to follow his ideals despite the overwhelming threats to them—threats that have originated in his own family and from his own actions.

The king and queen of *Camelot* are very much like their counterparts in White's novels. Logan and Harris repeatedly stress Arthur's "ordinary" qualities to make him more likable and sympathetic. His first song, "I Wonder What the King Is Doing Tonight," reveals his fear of meeting Guenever and his larger fear of women in general: "You mean the appalling clamoring / That sounds like a blacksmith hammering / Is merely the banging of his royal knees? Please!" Even the world's most famous monarch shakes at the thought of being embarrassed in front of a beautiful woman. When Arthur meets Guenever (on the road to Camelot), he is able to speak with her only because she does not know that he is the King; like Shakespeare's King Henry V, Arthur enjoys momentary anonymity and escaping the burden of his crown. Guenever is introduced as a soon-to-be medieval "trophy wife," protesting that she "won't be bid and bargained for like beads at a bazaar" and asking, in song, "Where Are the Simple Joys of Maidenhood?" Her song, however, proves ironic when she asks in it, "Shall two knights never tilt for me / And let their blood be spilt for me?" and "Shall a feud not begin for me?" Like Arthur, she proves endearing to the audience, who already knows the story and is therefore touched by the irony of her naiveté.

An interesting departure from White's version of the myth is Guenever's initial reaction to Lancelot. Unlike many Hollywood love stories, *Camelot* does not include a scene where the lovers' eyes first meet and lock. Instead, the queen finds Lancelot's pride "overbearing" and his boasting "pretentious": When he brags of his having achieved physical perfection, she remarks, "Tell me, have you jousted with humility lately? Or is *humilitie* not in fashion in France this year?" When Arthur defends Lancelot on the grounds that "He's a stranger! He's not even English! He's French!" Guenever quips, "Well, he suffers in translation." (Pellinore also shares Guenever's suspicion of Lancelot's high morals when he asks Arthur, "Are you *sure* he's French?") Her distaste for Lancelot is made into a comic subplot in which she convinces three different knights to defeat Lancelot at an upcoming tournament. When Lancelot predictably defeats the first two, kills the third, and then performs a miracle by resurrecting him, she no longer doubts his holiness and instead becomes fascinated (and enamored) of him.

In both *The Ill-Made Knight* and *The Candle in the Wind*, Arthur remains willfully (and consciously) ignorant of Guenever's adultery for as long as he can sustain his own fantasy. White offers the reader a number of scenes in which Arthur hopes to "weather the trouble by refusing to become conscious of it." *Camelot*'s Arthur shares a similar attitude, expressed after he knights Lancelot without any joy and sees his best knight looking nervously at the queen. Like Hamlet, Arthur wanders the castle in a state of melancholy—and again like that Danish prince, he engages in a soliloquy, which begins in one emotional state—"I love them, and they answer me with pain and torment. Be it sin or not sin, they have betrayed me in their hearts and that's far sin enough . . . They must pay for it"—but concludes in quite another: "I'm a king, not a man, and a very civilized king. Could it possibly be civilized to destroy the thing I love? Could it possibly be civilized to love myself above all?"

What Arthur has done here is move from a wicked desire for revenge (which he later calls "the most worthless of causes") to a state of godliness. Arthur's God (of the Old Testament) proclaimed, "Vengeance is mine," and by forsaking the desire for vengeance and replacing it with a resolution to bring civilization to a people very much like himself, Arthur has proven himself better than his troubles.

After Arthur formulates this resolution, *Camelot* continues with the arrival of Mordred (who prompts Arthur to state, "The adage that 'blood is thicker than water' was invented by undeserving relatives"). Arthur's son accuses Guenever, and the queen is tried, found guilty, and sentenced to death. As he does in *The Candle in the Wind*, Mordred mocks his father's ideas of "justice" and raises the thorny legal issues that are such a large part of that novel: "Why not pardon her? But you can't do that, can you? Let her die—your life is over. Let her live—your life's a fraud. Kill the queen or kill the law." As in *The Candle in the Wind*, Guenever's rescue by Lancelot provokes Arthur into war but simultaneously spares him the pain of having to watch his wife burned at the stake.

Camelot concludes with a final meeting of the three main characters before Arthur's attack on Joyous Gard. Lancelot and Guenever beg Arthur to take them back, but he refuses on the grounds that "the Table is dead." Arthur knows that his idea "exists no more" now that Lancelot and Guenever have begun a chain of events that have resulted in Arthur's knights "cheerful to be at war" and "those old uncivilized ways" that they "tried to put asleep forever" come back again. Arthur does not scorn them, however, but accepts the collapse of his dream as inevitable: He clasps Lancelot's hand firmly before he leaves and says "Goodbye, my love" to Guenever as she returns to her life as a Holy Sister. Arthur is at his lowest point—until, as in *The Candle in the Wind*, a young page named Tom Malory approaches Arthur and tells him that he wants to be a knight. The mood of the king—and of the film—changes, as

Arthur realizes that his attempt to use "Might for Right" need not have been in vain, as long as someone records what he has done to inspire future generations. Like himself, Tom Malory is "one of what we all are: Less than a drop in the great blue motion of sunlit sea, but it seems that some of the drops sparkle."

The Sword in the Stone (1963)

Directed by Wolfgang Reitherman; Screenplay by Bill Peet, based on T.H. White's novel; Featuring the voices of Rickie Sorensen (the Wart), Norman Alden (Kay), Sebastian Cabot (Sir Ector), Junius Matthews (Archimedes), and Karl Swenson (Merlyn).

The combination of Wolfgang Reitherman (who served as animation director for Disney's *Lady and the Tramp* and *Peter Pan*) and Bill Peet (who wrote the screenplays of *101 Dalmatians*, *Sleeping Beauty*, *Peter Pan*, and *Cinderella*) give their animated version of *The Sword in the Stone* the unmistakable Disney stamp. The film features songs, adventures in the woods, and a doe-eyed hero who (like Cinderella and Dumbo) overcomes adversity to prove triumphant at the film's end. While White's novel is presented in a much-simplified form, the film ultimately serves as a good introduction to its central issue—the value of education.

The familiar characters from White's novel all appear in this film, albeit in simplified versions in which their primary traits are exaggerated. The Wart is a feckless and scrawny twelve-year-old boy who maintains the same innocence that marked him in White's novel. Merlin, although still the Wart's tutor, is more bumbling and close to the cliched version of a wizard, casting spells that sound like gibberish ("Hockety Pockety Wockety Wack, / Abara Dabara Cabara Dack!") and getting his beard caught wherever it lands. Archimedes (Merlyn's owl) is a caricature of a know-it-all schoolmaster, constantly annoyed at his master and saying things like, "Pinfeathers!" The greatest departure in character lies in Sir Ector and Kay, who in this version resemble Cinderella's wicked stepsisters more than the two gruff (but ultimately good) figures that comprise Wart's adopted family in the novel. (The fact that they both have red hair while the Wart's is blonde stresses their difference in character from the kindhearted boy.) Much of what motivates the Wart, in fact, is proving his worth to these two overbearing figures. (The entire Robin Wood episode does not appear in the film, most likely so that Reitherman could keep its plot simple enough to grab young viewers.)

As in White's novel, Merlyn does transform the Wart into different animals; while these political science lessons-in-disguise make up a large part of the novel, however, the film only treats the Wart's transformation into three animals. The first is (as in the novel) a perch and although the Wart does not meet an animated version of Mr. P., he does get chased by a gigantic pike. As he swims in and out of weeds, trying to avoid being eaten, Merlyn sings a song about using your intellect. Merlyn's point here is that the Wart must use his brains instead of his brawn (which does not amount to much in the first place); after hearing the song, the Wart jams the pike's mouth open with a stick and swims to safety. Thus, his lesson was not an overtly political one, but rather one about the overall value of thinking.

The film then departs from White's novel by having Merlin transform the Wart into a squirrel. The wizard's logic in doing so is that the squirrel is "a tiny creature with enormous problems" and can therefore demonstrate to the boy how an alert mind (and agile feet) can help one stay alive. This sequence, however, soon becomes one played almost wholly for laughs when a female squirrel approaches the Wart and begins flirting with him in her chattering squirrel-talk. As the Wart runs from her advances, Merlin sings about the incomprehensibility of love.

After they change back into people, Merlin tells the Wart that love is stronger than gravity and "the greatest force on earth." No mention, however, is made of Guenever (or even marriage in general), again probably to keep the plot as simple as possible for a young audience.

The final transformation shown in the film is one in which the Wart becomes not a hawk or wild goose, but a sparrow. Archimedes teaches the boy to fly, which he does very well until he wanders into the cottage of Madam Mim, a mad and hideous sorceress appearing in the first version of *The Sword in the Stone* (before he revised it as part of *The Once and Future King*). Merlyn attempts to rescue the Wart, but is instead challenged by Madam Mim to a wizard's duel in which (in true cartoon fashion) she and Merlyn transform into a number of creatures. Merlyn finally wins the contest when he turns himself into a germ and gives Madam Mim an unpronounceable (yet not deadly) disease. Merlyn tells the Wart that the duel "was worth it if you learned something from it," and its lesson was clear: Merlyn played only defensively—for example, turning himself into a mouse after Madam Mim turned herself into an elephant. The fact that Merlyn won the duel as a creature no bigger than a germ again presses home the idea (central to White's entire series) that might is not always right.

The film ends in the same way as the novel: The Wart forgets Kay's sword at the London tournament and pulls the sword from the stone in order to cover his mistake. One difference is that the novel spans approximately seven years (making the Wart become King Arthur at 17 or 18 years of age), while the film spans less than a year—the Wart is still the Wart at the end of the film, sitting on a throne with his feet dangling in the air and his crown too large for his head. (Reitherman's reason for keeping the Wart a boy at the film's end may have to do with his wanting a younger audience to still identify with the Wart when he becomes King Arthur.) Regardless of these minor changes, the film presents a distilled version of the novels' main theme in a very palatable and direct manner.

First Knight (1995)

Directed by Jerry Zucker; Screenplay by Lorne Cameron, David Hoselton, and William Nicholson; Featuring Richard Gere (Lancelot), Sean Connery (King Arthur), Julia Ormond (Guenever), and Ben Cross (Prince Malagant).

While other film versions of the Arthurian saga attempt to reshape parts of the myth to further the issues explored by their directors, *First Knight* is different in its drastic alteration of several main parts of the plot. Mordred, for example, never appears (or even exists) and his father is killed in a battle with Prince Malagant (the film's land-grabbing villain) instead by his evil son. Arthur is an old, lonely man when he meets and weds Guenever—who herself has a degree of political power as the Lady of Lionesse. *First Knight*'s greatest departure from the myth, however, is its portrayal of Lancelot—instead of the conscience-stricken and suffering "ill-made knight" of both Malory and White's books, he behaves like a very cynical and modern man, pursuing Guenever without any initial cares about breaking his allegiances to Arthur or the Round Table. (He is not even French.) This is not to say that *First Knight* is a bad film, but simply that Jerry Zucker (its director) was interested in presenting a new, modern "spin" on the Arthurian love triangle.

Richard Gere plays Lancelot as a wisecracking and medieval version of a contemporary action-hero. In his first scene, he challenges anyone in a town square to duel with him for money; he defeats all comers by literally making their swords leap out of their hands. When a defeated opponent asks him his secret, Lancelot says, "You have to not care whether you live or die." Dueling for money is a most unchivalrous act, but Lancelot cares nothing for chivalry or status: After he saves Guenever from an ambush by Prince Malagant, he tells her that he would have rescued her as fast as if she were a dairymaid. When he meets her again, at a festival at Camelot, he runs the gauntlet (a deadly obstacle course with flying medicine balls, axes, and swords) in order to win a kiss from her—which he then refuses on the grounds that he "dare not kiss so lovely a lady." Like a leading man from any number of Hollywood romances, this Lancelot knows exactly what to say in order to convince even a queen that she wants to be with him. He brags that he has no master and does as he pleases—which is completely unlike his suffering and guilt-ridden counterpart in *The Ill-Made Knight*. Even King Arthur only receives the slightest of nods from Lancelot when the two are first introduced.

Guenever originally approaches her marriage as a political solution: Her village of Lionesse will soon be invaded by the marauding Prince Malagant and she thinks that marrying King Arthur will help her people gain the military protection they will need. Thus, she is not a helpless or confused young girl but is, like Lancelot, a very modern person with a clear idea of how politics work.

The fact that Sean Connery plays King Arthur lends an amount of gravity and charm to the part. He is older than one would expect King Arthur to be at the time of his wedding to Guenever, but what he lacks in youth he makes up for in stateliness and dignity: He tells Guenever that Camelot will still protect Lionesse even if she does not marry him. When Guenever responds that she does, in fact, want to be his wife, he asks her to honor the king, but love the man. His desire to marry is grounded partly in the loneliness that any King must feel as he is surrounded by people, few of which can speak freely to him.

Thus the three points of the love triangle are established, although how they begin to intersect is *First Knight*'s chief novelty. When Lancelot is invited by King Arthur to join the Round Table, Guenever speaks for him, saying that Lancelot is a free spirit and should be allowed to leave Camelot and "be free, with our love." However, Lancelot knows that she is saying this in order to keep him away from her (and thus removed as a temptation)—so he accepts King Arthur's offer, only as a means to get closer to Guenever. His knighting and pledges to his fellow knights ("Brother to brother, yours in life and death") therefore ring hollow, because Lancelot is speaking them to deceive everyone except Guenever, who knows exactly what he is doing.

Lancelot is not, however, only a wolf. The viewer learns that his cynicism and lack of genuine respect for the Round Table (or any institution other than himself) is the result of his childhood, during which he saw his family burned to death by attacking warlords as they hid in a church. As a result, Lancelot has nothing to lose and no set of beliefs. He lives according to chance and pursues Guenever simply because he wants her—and knows that she wants him. Luckily (for all involved), he and Guenever never physically consummate their love—they are caught in an embrace, by Arthur, who (through his behavior when threatened by Malagant) eventually inspires Lancelot to examine his own mercenary heart and recognize the value of defending a set of beliefs. The film therefore becomes the story of how this hard-edged and politically neutral man begins to believe in the ideals of the man that he originally wanted to betray. *The Ill-Made Knight* repeatedly stresses the fact that all three members of the love triangle love the other two equally; here, there is no great love between Arthur and Lancelot until the film's conclusion, at which time Lancelot is named "first knight" by the dying king. Watching Arthur's casket as it floats away, Lancelot raises his sword in a gesture of salute. Arthur has taught him, through his example, the credo that he has painted on the Round Table: "In serving each other, we become free." Lancelot is finally free of a life of detachment because Arthur has taught him about the value of service, sacrifice, and fighting for something higher than oneself—or one's own desires. Lancelot will become King after the film ends, making *First Knight*, like *The Sword in the Stone*, a story of transformation—in this case, from a cynic to a hero.

Monty Python and the Holy Grail (1975)

Directed by Terry Gilliam and Terry Jones; Screenplay by Graham Chapman, John Cleese, Terry Gilliam, Eric Idle, Terry Jones, and Michael Palin; Featuring Graham Chapman (King Arthur), John Cleese (Lancelot), Eric Idle (Robin), Terry Jones (Bedevere), and Michael Palin (Galahad)

Parody is the art of imitating an existing literary (or other artistic) form. Notable literary parodies include Jonathan Swift's *Gulliver's Travels*, Alexander Pope's *The Rape of the Lock*, and Tom Stoppard's *Rosencrantz and Guildenstern Are Dead*. Film is an art form that has greatly lent itself to parodists: Some famous examples of film parody are *Young Frankenstein*, *Airplane!*, *Austin Powers*, and *Monty Python and the Holy*

Grail, which stands as one of the most popular parodies of all time. Part of the film's appeal lies in its skewering the clichés of knighthood and chivalry that are familiar to many viewers through their reading of Malory and White. While a student of Arthurian legend will not learn any of "the official story" from this film, he or she will definitely learn about the conventions of knighthood through they ways in which they are parodied by the Python troupe.

The world of *Monty Python and the Holy Grail* is one that looks vaguely medieval (there are knights, kings, battles, lots of mud) but also surreal. Arthur and his knights do not ride horses, but instead skip while their servants bang two coconut halves in rhythm. God appears in the sky as a purposefully cheap-looking piece of animation and tells the knights to stop groveling ("Every time I try to talk to someone it's sorry this and forgive me that and I'm not worthy") before he tells them to search for the Grail. The film stops, rather than concludes, when a team of twentieth-century policemen finally catches up with Lancelot, who earlier in the film kills a "noted historian" as he explains Arthur's predicament to the audience. This combination of earnest, questing knights and an illogical and silly world is what gives the film much of its comedy.

Other laughs occur as a result of the Python troupe's ability to parody Arthurian legends. For example, the bravery knights are supposed to possess is constantly used as the basis for jokes. When the Black Knight fights Arthur for the right to cross a bridge, Arthur hacks off the Black Knight's arm—but the Black Knight keeps fighting, claiming his injury "'tis but a scratch." Arthur then proceeds to cut off the Black Knight's remaining arm—and both of his legs—while his adversary constantly says things like, "I've had worse!" and "Come on, you pansy!" The Black Knight's opposite is found in Sir Robin, a knight who (throughout the film) flees from danger, causing his minstrels to sing of his cowardice. King Arthur's most often-heard charge in the film is not, "Attack!" or "Defend the Round Table," but "Run away! Run away!"

Another source of parody is the knights' actual discovery of the Grail. To find it, they must first receive directions from a wizard named Tim— who tells them that they will have to enter the Cave of Caerbannog— a cave guarded by "a creature so foul" that the bones of "full fifty men lie strewn about its lair." When the knights arrive at the cave and learn that the creature described by Tim is a white rabbit, they are as surprised as the viewer. However, in the world of Monty Python, jokes come unexpectedly, and the rabbit leaps from knight to knight, ripping their heads off in a bloodbath so excessive and gory that it parodies both the traditional battles against dragons as well as other films which attempt to portray the violence of the Middle Ages in a "realistic" fashion. (The rabbit is killed not by Excalibur or a similarly "noble" weapon, but instead by the Holy Hand Grenade of Antioch.) When the knights finally see the Grail, on the other side of a bridge, they must answer the riddles of the bridgekeeper—a parody of Perceval's test in Malory. However, instead of being asked, "*What is the secret of the Grail?*" the knights are asked, "*What is your favorite color?*"—and some even manage to answer incorrectly.

Fans of the television show *Monty Python's Flying Circus* will recognize the fast and argumentative dialogue—over a presumably gruesome topic—as a Python trademark. More black humor occurs when Lancelot attempts to save a "maiden in distress" from a forced marriage: arriving at the reception, he kills so many of the guests in such a short amount of time that the effect is humorous instead of shocking. The violence found in *Le Morte D'Arthur*, *The Once and Future King*, and other works of Arthurian literature is exaggerated, making it more ridiculous than noble.

Throughout their film, the Python troupe obviously has no intention to offer its viewers any sort of moral instruction or debate about the rigors of knighthood. However, their enthusiasm for Arthurian legends is apparent in every scene, because only people who intensely loved the stories in the first place can know them well enough to parody them so effectively.

CliffsNotes Review

Use this CliffsNotes Review to test your understanding of the original text, and reinforce what you've learned in this book. After you work through the essay questions and useful practice projects, you're well on your way to understanding a comprehensive and meaningful interpretation of *The Once and Future King*.

Identify the Quote

1. "We can't have the boys runnin' about all day like hooligans—after all, damn it all? Ought to be havin' a first-rate eddication, at their age."

2. "Seventeen years ago, come Michaelmas, and been after the Questing Beast ever since. Boring, very."

3. "But I unfortunately was born at the wrong end of time, and I have to live backwards in front, while surrounded by a lot of people living forwards from behind."

4. "Education is experience, and the essence of experience is self-reliance."

5. "EVERYTHING NOT FORBIDDEN IS COMPULSORY."

6. "But what creature could be so low as to go about in bands, to murder others of its own blood?"

7. "Please get up, Sir Ector, and don't make everything so horrible. Oh, dear, oh, dear, I wish I had never seen that filthy sword at all."

Answers: (1) Sir Ector. (2) King Pellinore. (3) Merlyn. (4) Merlyn. (5) Sign in the ant colony. (6) Lyo-Lyok, the wild goose. (7) the Wart.

Essay Questions

1. Compose an essay comparing and contrasting the Wart and Kay's development as characters. What characteristics do they share? How does White make them seem both similar and dissimilar to the reader?

2. Describe the different father figures found in the novel. How does each figure contribute to the Wart's maturity?

3. Compare and contrast White's version of Arthur's childhood with Malory's. What aspects of the young king's personalities do both writers stress? How are the portrayals different?

4. Compare and contrast White's version of the Arthur saga with any Arthurian films.

5. Discuss how the Wart is like other youthful literary protagonists, such as Tom Sawyer, Huckleberry Finn, or Holden Caulfield.

6. Compose an essay in which you trace the development of Arthur's character through any two successive volumes of *The Once and Future King*.

7. Compare Arthur to any other literary hero, such as Beowulf or Odysseus. What heroic qualities do the figures share?

8. Read the poem *Sir Gawain and the Green Knight* and explain how it teaches the reader the values and assumptions behind chivalry.

9. Describe in what ways White's is novel like a beast fable by Aesop. Consider the use of animals for the teaching of morals.

10. Choose any two minor characters (such as King Pellinore or the Dog Boy) and explain how they contribute to any of the novel's main themes.

Practice Projects

1. Write a chapter from the novel in which the Wart is transformed into an animal not found in the book. Be sure to explain (through dialogue or a lecture by Merlyn) how this transformation helps further the Wart's education.

2. If you are familiar with HTML or other means of Web-site design, create an interactive Web site that teaches its users about the Arthurian legends.

3. Imagine that you are making a new film version of *The Sword in the Stone* (or other volumes of *The Once and Future King*). Write about who you would cast in what roles. Justify your choices.

CliffsNotes Resource Center

The learning doesn't need to stop here. CliffsNotes Resource Center shows you the best of the best—links to the best information in print and online about the author and/or related works. And don't think that this is all we've prepared for you; we've put all kinds of pertinent information at www.cliffsnotes.com. Look for all the terrific resources at your favorite bookstore or local library and on the Internet. When you're online, make your first stop www.cliffsnotes.com where you'll find more incredibly useful information about *The Once and Future King*.

Books and Articles

This CliffsNotes book, published by IDG Books Worldwide, Inc., provides a meaningful interpretation of *The Once and Future King*. If you are looking for information about the author and/or related works, check out these other publications:

BERGER, THOMAS. *Arthur Rex: A Legendary Novel*. New York: Delacorte Press, 1978.

CRANE, JOHN K. *T. H. White*. Boston: Twayne Publishers, 1974.

DAY, DAVID. *The Search for King Arthur*. New York: Facts on File, Inc., 1995.

MALORY, SIR THOMAS. *Le Morte D'Arthur*. New York: The Modern Library, 1999.

MINARY, RUTH AND CHARLES MOORMAN. *An Arthurian Dictionary*. Chicago: Academy Chicago Publishers, 1990.

SHEPHERD, KENNETH R. "T. H. White." *Contemporary Authors New Revision Series*. Gen. ed. James G. Lesniak. Volume 37. Detroit: Gale Research Inc., 1992. 464–67.

WARNER, SYLVIA TOWNSEND. *T. H. White: A Biography*. New York: The Viking Press, 1967.

WHITE, T.H. *The Once and Future King*. New York: G. P. Putman's Sons, 1958.

WHITE, T.H. *The Book of Merlyn*. Austin: University of Texas Press, 1977.

WHITE, T.H. *The Sword in the Stone* (original version). New York: G. P. Putman's Sons, 1939.

It's easy to find books published by IDG Books Worldwide, Inc. You'll find them in your favorite bookstores (on the Internet and at a store near you). We also have three web sites that you can use to read about all the books we publish:

* www.cliffsnotes.com

* www.dummies.com

* www.idgbooks.com

Internet

Check out these Web resources for more information about King Arthur and T.H. White.

The Avalon Archives, http://www.geocities.comAthens/Aegean/3780/avalon/avalon.html—links to Arthurian books, reviews, artwork, and other sites.

The Camelot Project at the University of Rochester, http://www.lib.rochester.edu/camelot/cphome.stm—contains a database of a database of Arthurian texts, images, and bibliographies.

"England Have My Bones:" For the Reader of the Works of T. H. White, http://www2.netdoor.com/~moulder/thwhite.html—a site dedicated to the readership of the literary works of T.H. White.

King Arthur: The Stuff of Future Memory, http://www.angelfire.com/ia/camelot—provides text and artwork of Authurian legends.

Le Morte D'Arthur: Thomas Malory's Book of King Arthur and His Noble Knights of the Round Table, http://etext.lib.virginia.edu—allows for text and word searches of passages or words from *Le Morte D'Arthur*.

The Mystic Realm of King Arthur, http://www.public.iastate.edu/~camelot/arthur.html—gives superb information on electronic links, teaching guides and publications, and the latest discussions on Arthurian legends.

Next time you're on the Internet, don't forget to drop by `www.cliffsnotes.com`. We've created an online Resource Center that you can use today, tomorrow, and beyond.

Index

CliffsNotes

LITERATURE NOTES

Absalom, Absalom!
The Aeneid
Agamemnon
Alice in Wonderland
All the King's Men
All the Pretty Horses
All Quiet on the
    Western Front
All's Well &
    Merry Wives
American Poets of the
    20th Century
American Tragedy
Animal Farm
Anna Karenina
Anthem
Antony and Cleopatra
Aristotle's Ethics
As I Lay Dying
The Assistant
As You Like It
Atlas Shrugged
Autobiography of
    Ben Franklin
Autobiography of
    Malcolm X
The Awakening
Babbit
Bartleby & Benito
    Cereno
The Bean Trees
The Bear
The Bell Jar
Beloved
Beowulf
The Bible
Billy Budd & Typee
Black Boy
Black Like Me
Bleak House
Bless Me, Ultima
The Bluest Eye & Sula
Brave New World
The Brothers Karamazov

The Call of the Wild &
    White Fang
Candide
The Canterbury Tales
Catch-22
Catcher in the Rye
The Chosen
The Color Purple
Comedy of Errors...
Connecticut Yankee
The Contender
The Count of
    Monte Cristo
Crime and Punishment
The Crucible
Cry, the Beloved
    Country
Cyrano de Bergerac
Daisy Miller &
    Turn...Screw
David Copperfield
Death of a Salesman
The Deerslayer
Diary of Anne Frank
Divine Comedy-I.
    Inferno
Divine Comedy-II.
    Purgatorio
Divine Comedy-III.
    Paradiso
Doctor Faustus
Dr. Jekyll and Mr. Hyde
Don Juan
Don Quixote
Dracula
Electra & Medea
Emerson's Essays
Emily Dickinson Poems
Emma
Ethan Frome
The Faerie Queene
Fahrenheit 451
Far from the Madding
    Crowd
A Farewell to Arms
Farewell to Manzanar
Fathers and Sons
Faulkner's Short Stories

Faust Pt. I & Pt. II
The Federalist
Flowers for Algernon
For Whom the Bell Tolls
The Fountainhead
Frankenstein
The French
    Lieutenant's Woman
The Giver
Glass Menagerie &
    Streetcar
Go Down, Moses
The Good Earth
The Grapes of Wrath
Great Expectations
The Great Gatsby
Greek Classics
Gulliver's Travels
Hamlet
The Handmaid's Tale
Hard Times
Heart of Darkness &
    Secret Sharer
Hemingway's
    Short Stories
Henry IV Part 1
Henry IV Part 2
Henry V
House Made of Dawn
The House of the
    Seven Gables
Huckleberry Finn
I Know Why the
    Caged Bird Sings
Ibsen's Plays I
Ibsen's Plays II
The Idiot
Idylls of the King
The Iliad
Incidents in the Life of
    a Slave Girl
Inherit the Wind
Invisible Man
Ivanhoe
Jane Eyre
Joseph Andrews
The Joy Luck Club
Jude the Obscure

Julius Caesar
The Jungle
Kafka's Short Stories
Keats & Shelley
The Killer Angels
King Lear
The Kitchen God's Wife
The Last of the
    Mohicans
Le Morte d'Arthur
Leaves of Grass
Les Miserables
A Lesson Before Dying
Light in August
The Light in the Forest
Lord Jim
Lord of the Flies
The Lord of the Rings
Lost Horizon
Lysistrata & Other
    Comedies
Macbeth
Madame Bovary
Main Street
The Mayor of
    Casterbridge
Measure for Measure
The Merchant
    of Venice
Middlemarch
A Midsummer Night's
    Dream
The Mill on the Floss
Moby-Dick
Moll Flanders
Mrs. Dalloway
Much Ado About
    Nothing
My Ántonia
Mythology
Narr. ...Frederick
    Douglass
Native Son
New Testament
Night
1984
Notes from the
    Underground

CliffsNotes™
@ cliffsnotes.com

Check Out the All-New CliffsNotes Guides

TECHNOLOGY TOPICS

PERSONAL FINANCE TOPICS

CAREER TOPICS